from Wendy
Christmas 97

The
FINISHING TOUCHES

Table Decorations • Giftwrapping • Napkin Folding
Creative designs for special occasions

The
FINISHING
TOUCHES

Table Decorations • Giftwrapping • Napkin Folding
Creative designs for special occasions

JANET BRIDGE

LINDA BARKER

Thunder Bay
P·R·E·S·S

A SALAMANDER BOOK

© Salamander Books Ltd, 1993, 1995, 1996

This edition published in 1996 by
Thunder Bay Press
5880 Oberlin Drive, Suite 400
San Diego, CA 92121-9653

1 3 5 7 9 8 6 4 2

Thunder Bay Press Books are available for bulk purchase for sales promotion
and premium use. For details, write or call the manager of special sales
Thunder Bay Press
5880 Oberlin Drive, Suite 400
San Diego, California 92121-9653

ISBN 1-57145-036-X

All correspondence concerning the content of this volume
should be addressed to Salamander Books Ltd.

CREDITS

Table Decorations and Giftwrapping Designs: Janet Bridge

Napkin Folding Designs: Linda Barker

Managing Editors: Joanna Smith, Samantha Gray

Photographers: Simon Butcher, Graham Rae and Steve Tanner

Art Editor: Paul Johnson

Designer: Louise Bruce

Color Separation: P&W Graphics Pte Ltd, Singapore and Scantrans Pte Ltd, Singapore

Printed in Singapore

CONTENTS

TABLE DECORATIONS
11

The meal itself is important, but so too is creating pleasant surroundings and the right atmosphere, whether at a formal dinner party or a relaxed supper with family and close friends. The right table decorations can really set the scene and make a meal a truly memorable occasion. This section is packed with a host of table decorating ideas, including centerpieces, table cloths and mats, placecards, napkins and table gifts to delight your guests.

NAPKIN FOLDING
69

Folded or decorated napkins add a special finishing touch to meals and it is surprising just how many shapes you can create from a basic linen or paper square. This section features classic folds for elegant table settings and fun, informal designs for picnics or light meals – you can even make your own napkin rings. The designs are divided into decorative, formal and informal folds to help you make your choice.

GIFTWRAPPING
129

The more attractive and unique a gift looks, the greater the enjoyment – for both the giver and the receiver. Beautiful giftwrapping will make more of a gift, and make the occasion special for all involved. This section demonstrates nearly 50 stylish designs using papers, fabrics, boxes, and bags, with ideas for gift tags and extra trimmings to add a finishing touch.

Index
188

PART ONE

TABLE DECORATIONS

Introduction

12

Centerpieces

15

Tablecloths & Mats

33

Napkins, Gifts & Placecards

47

INTRODUCTION

Appliqué tablemats are simple to make and
can be used many times to create different
effects with other decorations on the table.

As the cost of eating in restaurants increases and home cooking becomes more adventurous, entertaining at home has become an enjoyable pastime for many people. Arranging your home to welcome your guests is part of the preparation; the warmth of the welcome and the atmosphere you have created adds to the enjoyment of the occasion. The amount of money you spend is immaterial. It is the presentation that really counts. If you have spent some time and effort your guests will appreciate the thought you have put in and enjoy themselves from the moment they step through the door. Obviously the meal itself is important but so too is creating a visually pleasing setting and the right atmosphere whether at a formal dinner party or a relaxed supper with a few friends.

Fresh flowers have always been a popular way of dressing a table and are suitable for any occasion. When you make an arrangement, though, do take into consideration the amount of space available. Only too often, pretty centerpieces have to be moved to make space for serving dishes. Also, the height has to be taken into consideration. There is nothing more frustrating than not being able to see your fellow diners across the table and it makes conversation very difficult. The obvious way to get over this difficulty is to keep a flower arrangement low, but another option is to stand it on a pedestal. I have included an arrangement on a pedestal cakestand (see page 18) to show you how to do this. Alternatively, instead of having one large arrangement in the center of the table, why not have a series of smaller arrangements around the table?

When choosing flowers for an arrangement, there are many factors to consider. You may wish to select colors to match your crockery or the decor in your dining room or even complement the food you are serving. The occasion may also be a consideration. For instance, you may wish to set the scene with red roses for a romantic dinner for two, but it would be better to choose lots of pretty white flowers for a family gathering. Whatever the occasion, look around the garden or in the florist's shop to see what is available and remember to avoid poisonous plants.

Candlelit Meals

There is nothing quite like the warm, soft glow of a candle and rarely can it be created any other way. The soft pools of light create an intimate atmosphere which is very flattering to the faces around the table. There are numerous types of candle available in all colors, shapes, and sizes. Alter candles are ever popular, while floating candles are a relatively new idea and are now available in a range of different designs and colors. When combined with a few fresh flower heads, they make an effective floating arrangement for the center of the table; choose the flowers to complement the occasion. Outdoor candles are also now readily available and are perfect for warm summer evenings. If any wax spills on the tablecloth, scrape off the excess with a knife then cover the mark with brown paper or kitchen towel and press with a warm iron. Remove any remaining color with methylated spirit but check the cloth for colorfastness first.

Below: This elegant centerpiece will scent the room with a soft, flowery fragrance and will go on giving pleasure well after the meal.

Above: The tradition of presenting gifts at the table is a long and happy one. These spice tins are one of the many gift ideas in this book.

Choosing Crockery

If the crockery you purchase is going to be used every day, then it is advisable not to spend too much money and to check whether it is dishwasherproof, if necessary. The choice is endless and there are so many styles and patterns now available that it ultimately comes down to personal preference. However, I have found that a plainer design is more versatile, because it can be dressed up to create whatever style you like. The addition of a checked tablecloth and cotton napkins tied with gingham ribbon, for instance, makes a homey, country style, while using the same china on a bold tablecloth with brightly-striped napkins can create a thoroughly contemporary feel.

Remember that with careful thought and planning you can create a setting for any occasion whether it is inside or out, summer or winter, formal or informal. I hope the ideas in this book will help you to do this and inspire you to devise schemes of your own.

Below: These dainty fabric bags are a lovely way of presenting mints or other candies to your guests to eat after the meal.

Right: A simple posy of wheat ears and dried flowers on each side plate lifts a plain table into a pretty, thoughtful scheme.

CHAPTER ONE

CENTERPIECES

A centerpiece is a must for every table, whether
it is at a formal dinner or a buffet. Creating a focal point will help add
balance to the scheme. Any of the ideas in this section will certainly provide
the first topic for conversation among your guests.

Christmas Cone Basket

1 Cut the foliage into short lengths and strip the ends to create a stem on each. Wrap a wire around the base of each cone, twist the ends together and leave one end long. Lightly spray a few of the cones with gold paint.

2 Wire three plastic oasis holders onto the base of the basket and push a thoroughly soaked oasis onto them. Insert a thick layer of foliage around the oasis to create a good base for the arrangement. Push two candles into the oasis.

3 Add cones and more of the foliage to the arrangement, working your way from the base to the top, making sure the oasis is well covered. Add gold cherubs, wired ribbon bows and twigs as finishing touches if you have them.

Harvest Roses

1 Glue two oasis holders to the base of the basket and push a block of dry oasis on top to fit snugly into the basket. Spread glue around the rim of the basket and press dry sphagnum moss onto it. Trim off any long ends.

2 Trim the dried wheat, leaving 2in (5cm) of stem on each ear. Working from the basket handle to the edges, insert the wheat stems into the foam close together so the foam is not visible, leaving a narrow margin around the sides.

3 Trim the stems of some dried roses to a similar length and insert into the oasis around the edges of the basket, with their heads resting on the rim. Use tweezers to hold the stems to prevent damaging them.

Cakestand Centerpiece

1 You need a soaked oasis ring which fits on your cakestand. Start by cutting the conifer foliage into short lengths and strip the ends of the stems. Insert around the outside edge of the ring and repeat in the center with shorter pieces.

2 When the foliage ring is complete, cut the stems of the flowers and the other types of foliage to the right length. Build up the flower ring, adding extra foliage between them to create softness. Aim to achieve a good balance of color.

3 Place the ring on the cakestand and make any necessary adjustments. Add a few stems of trailing ivy and some extra flowers hanging down below the rim of the stand to make a graceful cascade around all sides.

Terracotta Candlepots

1 Line the base of a small terracotta flowerpot with dry oasis foam. Stand the candle on the foam and check it is at the right height. Cut further pieces of oasis to fit around the candle and hold it securely in place.

2 Start to add the dried flowers around the candle. Begin with a thick ring of deep pink, dyed flowers. Leave the stems quite long so they will stand up above the outer flowers and remain visible around the candle.

3 Next add florets of dried pink hydrangea, filling up the space and allowing the outer flowers to hang down over the edge of the pot. Finish with a few dried nigella seedheads at intervals to add extra interest.

Citrus Ring

1 Snip off some evenly-sized laurel leaves and insert them around the edges of a soaked oasis ring. Repeat with some smaller leaves around the inside edge of the ring.

2 Attach wires to a selection of fruits so they can be inserted into the ring. Insert wires through the bases of the large fruits and twist the long ends together, but make wire staples for the smaller fruits and push them right through.

3 Build up the arrangement by adding the large fruits first and adding the smaller ones between them. Add extra leaves to fill any gaps. The fruit must not be eaten from this centerpiece, it is purely decorative.

Spring Garden

1 Take a shallow terracotta bowl and line the base with gravel to increase drainage. Next fill the bowl with potting soil and firm lightly. Choose a few pots of spring plants such as primroses, snowdrops, dwarf daffodils, and ivies.

2 Remove the plants from their pots and gently set into the soil, arranging them evenly around the bowl to give a balanced appearance. Firm the soil around them and add more if necessary. Water lightly.

3 Cover the surface of the soil with moss. Terracotta is porous, so you will need to stand a mat under the bowl to protect your table. If you wish to keep the plants after the meal, take them out of the bowl and repot them as they were before.

Buffet Table Display

 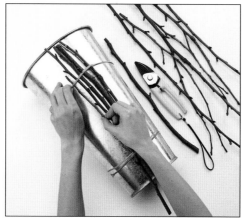 

1 Wrap three elastic bands around a tall galvanized bucket 4in (10cm) from the top rim. Repeat with another three 4in (10cm) from the bottom rim.

2 Trim down a number of straight twigs and slip them under the elastic bands. Arrange them close together and continue around the bucket until the outside is covered.

3 Use two thick bundles of raffia to tie around the bucket and cover the elastic bands. Use short pieces to tie the raffia bundles to the elastic bands. Fill the bucket with sunflowers.

Dried Bean Plate

1 Draw around your dish onto a sheet of tracing paper, then draw a pattern on the paper. Using the pattern as a guide, paint each area of the plate in turn with glue and stick the larger beans to it in neat rows using your fingers.

2 Stick a line of large beans around the areas that you are going to fill with smaller legumes such as couscous or small lentils. Paint the area with glue and then pour the legumes on top. Press then shake off the ones that haven't stuck.

3 A star outlined in black peppercorns makes a strong centerpiece for the design. We filled in all the space around it with yellow split peas to set it off. When the design is complete and the glue is dry, give the dish three coats of varnish.

Gilded Fruit Basket

1 Using a glue gun, stick together a selection of different nuts to make small clusters. Once the glue is dry, lightly spray the nuts with gold paint using an aerosol.

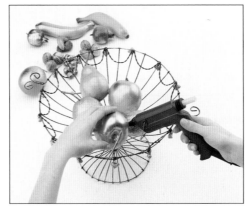

2 Next spray a selection of artificial fruits with the gold paint, aiming for just a light covering to allow the colors of the fruits to show through. Lay some of the fruit in the basket to create a firm base, gluing it together as you go.

3 Continue to add the fruit and the clusters of nuts until the arrangement is complete. As a finishing touch, lightly spray a stem of artificial ivy and wind among the fruit.

Scented Bowl

1 Wire together a small posy of dried lavender, dried miniature roses and dried gypsophila, creating separate layers of color. Repeat to make four posies in all and trim the stems of each.

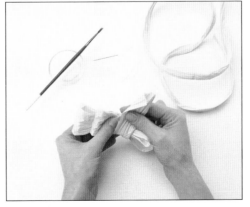

2 To make the bows, take a piece of paper ribbon and fold both ends into the center to make two loops; sew or stick into place. Repeat with a shorter length and attach on top. Make the knot by wrapping a short piece around the center.

3 Stick a mound of florist's putty on each end of the bowl and push two bundles of dried flowers into them, with the stems facing each other. Once the putty has dried, use a strong adhesive to stick a bow at each end to cover it.

Jeweled Vases

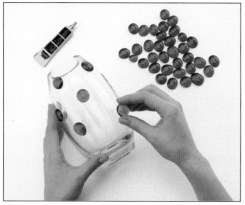

1 Using an extra strong adhesive, glue colored glass nuggets onto the outside of a clear glass vase. You may have to do one side at a time and allow the glue to dry before you start on the other side.

2 Decorate the spaces between the nuggets with spots of gold glass paint and leave until completely dry.

3 Choose flowers which will complement the color and style of the vase, such as these bold tulips and bright daffodils.

Fruit Bags

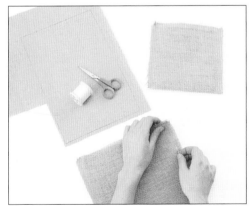

1 Cut out four burlap rectangles 4x10in (10x25cm) and six 8x12in (20x30cm). Fold each in half, right sides facing, and machine- or handstitch up both sides to create ten little burlap bags.

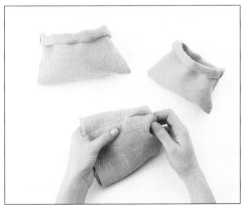

2 Turn the bags through, taking care to push the corners out square. Fold the tops of the bags over and roll to about halfway down the sides.

3 Fill the bags with a selection of different fruits that your guests can enjoy after the meal, either as a dessert or with their coffee. Arrange the bags on a tray or in an open basket.

Ice Salad Bowl

1 Take two bowls, one 3in (8cm) smaller in diameter than the other. Place the small bowl inside the large one and fill the gap between them with water. Stand a heavy weight in the small bowl and tape across the top to hold in place.

2 Place the bowls in the freezer, and when the water starts to turn to ice, remove from the freezer and slide slices of fruit and sprigs of herbs and foliage into the iced water, pushing them well down between the bowls. Return to the freezer.

3 When the water has frozen completely, take out of the freezer and remove the weight and adhesive tape. Stand the bowls into a basin of cold water and pour more water into the small bowl; the two will eventually come apart.

Cellophane Bouquet

1 Strip the lower leaves from the flowers and foliage. Take 10 to 15 stems and tie tightly together in a bunch. Then add the other stems around the central bunch, at a slight angle to make a neat spiral. Tie and trim the stems level.

2 Lay the bouquet on a large sheet of cellophane and bring the sides up over the flowers. Stick the edges together with adhesive tape, then gather the cellophane tightly around the stems and tie in place. Trim the cellophane level with the stems.

3 Lay two squares of cellophane, one on top of the other. Place the stems in the center and bring all the edges up around the flowers. Gather around the stems and tie tightly. Pour water between the flowers to fill up the "bag" at the base.

Floating Flower Heads

1 Wrap a large elastic band around a shallow glass bowl. Trim the stems from some large ivy leaves and slip the leaves under the band, making a neat row right around the bowl.

2 Tie a narrow ribbon around the bowl to cover the elastic band and finish in a bow. Fill the bowl with water.

3 Snip the heads off some flowers and float them in the bowl. We have chosen white chrysanthemums and asters, but roses will also look very effective. Add a few floating candles and light them just before the meal.

Sunflower Wreath

1 Take a handful of hay and lay it on a flat 10in (25cm) wire ring. Wire in place and repeat until the ring is covered. Tie pieces of raffia around the ring at intervals to cover the wire and hold the hay close to the ring to form a neat circle.

2 Make four small posies using some strands of hay, ears of wheat, artificial sunflowers and a few dried flowers. The posies should have flat backs and a similar arrangement of materials in each. Hold the stems together with wire.

3 Tie the posies to the hay base with raffia and finish with a bow. Space them equally around the ring, all facing the same way. This would make a lovely centerpiece for a summer lunch, indoors or out.

Miniature Rose Basket

1 Wrap some long trails of ivy around the rim of the basket and hold them in place with wire which can be threaded backward and forward through the wicker in a stitching action. Line the basket with polythene.

2 Half fill the basket with potting soil, remove the roses from their pots and arrange on the soil. Add more soil to fill the gaps between the rootballs of the plants and firm lightly around them.

3 Water the soil until just moist, then cover the surface with moss until the soil is no longer visible. If you wish to keep the roses after the meal, take them out of the basket and repot into their original containers.

CHAPTER TWO

TABLECLOTHS & MATS

Tablecloths and mats form the basis of the scheme upon which you can
build the other elements. Once you have made the cloths and mats in this section
you can use them time and again, perhaps combining them with different
centerpieces, napkins, or crockery for a range of different effects.

Plaid Table Setting

1 Cut two pieces of green fabric and one piece of thin wadding 17x14in (43x35cm). On the front of one piece of the fabric, arrange two pieces of plaid ribbon so they form a cross in one corner and sew in place. Sew matching piping along both edges of both pieces of ribbon.

2 Next cover a ¾in (2cm) button with green fabric. Cut an 8in (20cm) length of ribbon and sew the ends together. Sew small running stitches right around one edge of the ribbon and pull tight to gather up. Oversew to secure. Sew the button and tassel in the center of the rosette.

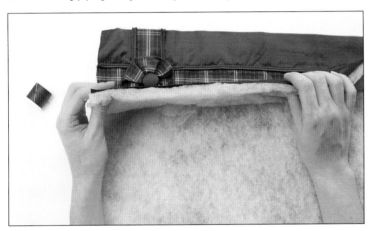

3 Sew the rosette onto the fabric where the ribbons cross. Arrange the two pieces of fabric right sides together and lay the wadding on top. Sew the three layers together right around the edges, leaving a small opening. Turn through and press. Slipstitch the opening.

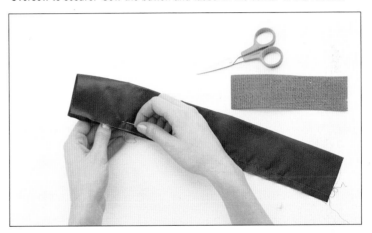

4 To make the napkin ring, cut a piece of stiffening 2x8in (5x20cm). Next cut a piece of the green fabric 5x16in (13x40cm) and fold in half, right sides together, down the length. Sew the long edges together, turn through and press.

5 Slide the fabric tube onto the piece of stiffening, gathering it up as you go. Bring the ends of the stiffening around together and overlap by ½in (1cm); sew in place. Fold under the raw ends of the fabric and sew together. Adjust the fabric to make the gathering even.

6 Make a rosette as before, but cut down the width of the ribbon by ½in (1cm) before you start, to make the rosette smaller. Attach a button and tassel in the same way and sew onto the napkin ring.

Appliqué Mat

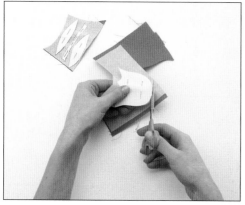

1 Draw a flower design on a sheet of paper and cut out the elements to make templates. Iron an adhesive backing onto some fabric remnants, then pin the templates onto them. Cut out the flower, stem, and leaf shapes.

2 Cut out a piece of fabric 7in (18cm) square. Arrange the flower pieces on it, remove the backing paper and iron them in place. Sew around the edges of all the pieces using blanket stitch for a decorative effect.

3 Fold a ½in (1cm) seam around all sides of the square of fabric and press to hold. Position the fabric in the center of the tablemat and pin, then sew, into place. Finish by adding a cross of red thread at each corner.

Fresh Flower Garlands

1 These garlands hang gracefully around the sides of a table; you can position the flowers at the corners of a square table or loop them evenly around the edges of a circular table. Tie thread around the muslin where you want them to be.

2 Make up a series of similar bouquets using a range of fresh flowers chosen to suit the occasion. Remember that the flowers will only be visible from one side and they will be hanging upside down. Wire the stems together.

3 Wire the bouquets to the muslin where you have marked with thread. Cover the wires with a large ribbon bow. Attach the muslin swags to the tablecloth by using safety pins or by sewing on behind each bouquet.

Gold Star Scheme

1 Draw three different-sized stars on paper and cut out. Cut a potato in half and pin a paper star on the cut surface. Cut around the star with a craft knife then cut away the excess potato, leaving the star sticking up in the center. Place face down on kitchen paper and repeat with the other stars.

2 Using a small paintbrush, apply a generous amount of gold fabric paint onto a potato star and make a print on a white tablecloth. Apply more paint to the potato and print another star on top of the first, turning the potato slightly to get a 10-sided star. Repeat with stars of different sizes.

3 When the cloth is covered with a random pattern of different-sized stars, make a set of napkins to match. Cut out 18in (45cm) squares of white fabric and hem all the raw edges. Either print the napkins with a random pattern of gold stars as before or just print one star in the center.

4 To make a napkin ring, cut a length of gold cord about 16in (40cm) long. Bind both ends of the gold cord tightly with gold thread to prevent them from fraying.

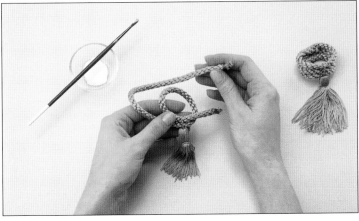

5 Take a gold tassel and thread the cord through the loop at the top. Take the end of the cord around in a circle and thread through the loop again. Repeat until you have three neat circles of gold cord threaded through the tassel loop. Tuck the ends in at the back and glue to the inside of the ring.

6 Lay the table and position the crockery and centerpiece. When everything is in place, sprinkle the center of the table with gold glitter to add a sparkle to the scheme.

Gingham Setting

1 Cut a rectangle of gingham fabric 16x12in (40x30cm) for each tablemat. Remove some of the threads from each of the short ends to leave a fringe about 1in (2.5cm) deep. Hem the long sides to keep the edges neat.

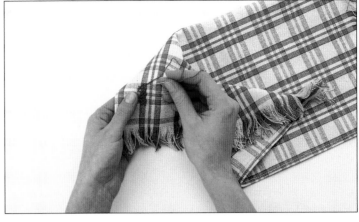

2 Using red embroidery thread, cross-stitch a simple heart motif in the top left-hand corner of each mat.

3 To make a napkin ring, cut a piece of gingham 14x3in (35x7.5cm). Fray the ends by 1in (2.5cm) as before then fold in half lengthway, right sides facing, and sew the long edges together. Trim the seam, turn through, and press.

4 To make a salt dough heart mix 2 tablespoons of plain flour, 1 tablespoon of salt, 1 teaspoon of vegetable oil and 2 tablespoons of water. Mix the ingredients thoroughly, then knead for about 5 minutes until you reach a smooth, firm consistency.

5 Roll out the dough on a floured surface to about ¼in (½cm) thick. Cut out small hearts with a pastry cutter or knife and make a hole in each with the end of a drinking straw. Transfer to a cookie sheet lined with waxed paper and bake in a cool oven for two hours.

6 When the hearts have cooled down, paint with red acrylic paint. Take a gingham napkin ring and tie in a loose knot. Using red embroidery thread, sew a salt dough heart on the knot of the napkin ring to hold it in place, passing the thread through the hole in the heart.

Bluebell Tablecloth

1 Draw a bluebell design on a piece of thin cardboard and cut it out using a sharp craft knife to make a stencil. The design can be as simple or as complicated as you like; you could even trace your design from another picture.

2 Lay your stencil on the tablecloth and draw around it lightly with a pencil to create the flower shape. Repeat at intervals all over the cloth, varying the angle for added interest.

3 Paint the flowers using fabric paints. Again, you can make the painting as simple or detailed as you wish depending on how experienced a painter you are. Once dry, press the cloth on the reverse side to "set" the paint.

Braid-edged Overcloth

1 Pin the piping cord around the edges of the cloth, easing it neatly around the corners. The edge of the piping tape should meet the edge of the cloth, with the cord on the inside. Stitch in place and oversew the ends of the cord.

2 Lay the lining fabric on top of the cloth, right sides facing, with the cord between them. Stitch the layers together, keeping close to the outer edge of the cord and leaving a small opening. Turn through and slipstitch the opening.

3 Remove 6in (15cm) lengths of cord from the tape and sew the ends to prevent fraying. Tie into loose knots and sew in place. Thread the loop of a tassel through the middle of each knot and stitch one to each corner of the cloth.

Patchwork Mat

1 Draw a pattern of squares and triangles and color in. Cut out 2in (5cm) paper squares to correspond with your pattern and cut some in half to make the triangles. Cut out a 3in (7.5cm) square or triangle of fabric for each to match your pattern and tack onto the paper templates.

2 Sew the patchwork pieces together along all their edges, following your pattern as a guide to positioning them. Take out the tacking and paper and press. You will be left with raw edges around all sides of the rectangle that the shapes have formed.

3 To make a border, cut out two strips of fabric 1½in (4cm) wide and the length of the short sides of the patchwork. Sew them to the sides of the patchwork, right sides facing, then turn out and press. Repeat with the long sides, remembering to add the width of the short borders.

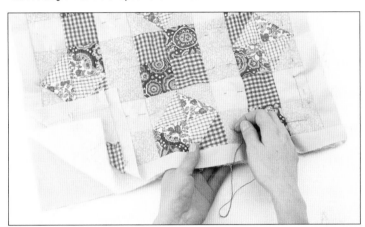

4 Cut a piece of fabric for the back of the mat and a piece of wadding the same size. Slip the wadding between the two pieces of fabric and pin the layers together. Next tack them in place, starting from the center using very large stitches all over the mat.

5 Quilt the triangles in the pattern by sewing small running stitches around all sides, ¼in (½cm) in from the edges through all layers. Remove the tacking stitches.

6 Cut four more 1½in (4cm) strips of fabric to form a binding around all sides of the mat. Lay onto the front of the mat, right sides facing, and stitch in place. Fold back and under the mat and stitch to the backing, enclosing all the raw edges. Repeat with the other three sides. Press the mat.

Seashell Mat

1 Take a length of soft cord and glue it around a plaited raffia tablemat, approximately 1in (2.5cm) from the edge.

2 Lay the shells on the mat with their edges butted up against the cord. It will be easier to arrange the shells evenly if you position the feature shells first, then fill in the gaps with cockle shells. Glue in place with a strong adhesive.

3 To make a matching napkin ring, glue a length of cord around a raffia-covered napkin ring. Place a shell on either side and glue securely in place.

CHAPTER THREE

NAPKINS, GIFTS & PLACECARDS

Thoughtful finishing touches, such as handmade placecards and napkin
rings of your own design can really make the meal a memorable occasion.
This section also includes bright ideas for presenting small gifts to
your guests at the table.

Fragrant Fruit Gifts

1 These are lovely, festive, scented gifts that your guests can take home to enjoy. Fill a small terracotta pot with dried oasis foam. Take a florist's spike and place it in the center of the oasis. Secure in place using wire staples.

2 Insert a ring of small laurel leaves into the foam all around the florist's spike to cover the foam and hang over the edges of the pot. Tie a piece of raffia around the florist's spike and finish with a bow. Fray the ends of the raffia.

3 Insert cloves into the orange to give it a spicy scent. If the skin is tough, pierce it with a darning needle first. Push the orange onto the florist's spike until it covers about half the spike and the raffia is still visible underneath.

Spice Tins

1 The spices are wrapped individually inside the tin. Cut off the corner of a plastic bag to make a pouch, fill with cloves and tie the top with string. Make a little bag from a fabric remnant, turn the top down and place the cloves inside.

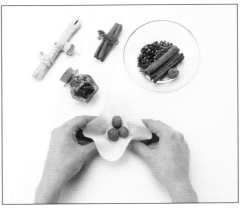

2 Tie a small bundle of cinnamon sticks together with orange raffia, then fill a tiny glass jar with peppercorns. Place three nutmegs in the center of a circle of muslin, bring up the sides then tie the top with fabric tape.

3 Arrange all the spices in the tin and add a few dried bay leaves to add to the decorative effect. Place the lid on the tin and wrap a long piece of fabric tape around the tin a number of times, finishing with a bow. Tuck two bay leaves under it.

Gingham Baskets

1 Take a small basket and partly fill with shredded wood. Cut a piece of gingham large enough to cover the shredded wood, tuck the edges underneath and push it down inside the basket, then glue in place.

2 Fill a miniature flowerpot with reindeer moss and glue in place. Add a few tiny dried flowers and glue them on top. Tie six ears of wheat together with raffia, trim the ends, and finish with a ribbon bow.

3 Arrange the flowerpot and wheat bundle in the basket. Add a loaf of miniature, artificial bread and a few dried or artificial flowers and glue into place. Your guests will welcome these keepsakes to remind them of the occasion.

Fruit Placecard Holder

1 To make the salt dough, follow the directions on page 41. First make the base by rolling a sausage shape, bringing the ends together to form an oval and flattening it. Make a selection of fruits and leaves and gently press onto the base.

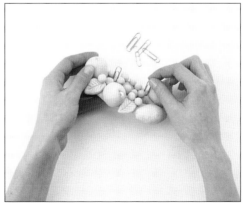

2 When the placecard holder is assembled and you are happy with the arrangement, take two paperclips and press them into the dough at the back of the holder so they stand upright and will hold a namecard.

3 Bake the placecard holder in a cool oven for at least two hours until baked through, then leave to cool. Paint the fruits and the base, adding as much detail as you like, then apply a spirit-based varnish to preserve the salt dough.

Pretty Mint Bags

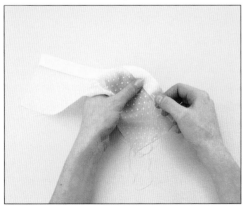

1 Cut a rectangle of sheer fabric 12x6in (30x15cm). Turn one of the long sides over by ¾in (2cm) and press. Turn it over again and tack, then sew, in place.

2 Fold the fabric in half with wrong sides facing. Sew down the side and along the bottom to form a bag. Trim the seam and turn inside out. Sew down the side and along the bottom again to enclose the raw edges inside.

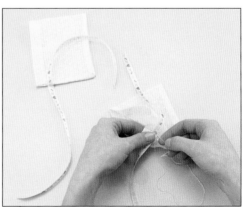

3 Turn the bag through again and press. Sew a length of ribbon to the side seam near the top of the bag. Fill with mints and tie the ribbon in a bow around the top of the bag. The mints can be eaten with coffee after the meal.

Chocolate Boxes

1 Draw a rectangle 2x2½in (5x6cm) on a piece of thin cardboard to form the base of the box. Add a 1½in (3cm) wide rectangle on each side of the base to form the sides of the box. Cut out, score around the base and fold up the sides.

2 Draw around the box on a sheet of patterned paper, adding an extra ½in (1cm) all around. Cut out and glue onto the outside of the box, overlapping the edges inside. Cover the inside with a piece of paper slightly smaller than the box.

3 Fold up the sides of the covered box and punch a hole in each corner. Tie the sides of the box together with ribbon to hold in place. Fill the box with shredded tissue paper and chocolates, for your guests to eat after the meal.

Potpourri Jars

1 Pick the flowers from some stems of dried gypsophila and grind in a mortar and pestle. Repeat with dried pink larkspur and blue delphinium and put to one side.

2 Other flowers can be snipped down to size with scissors. Use this technique with dried marigolds, achillea and mauve statice. Make sure the pieces are small or the petals will not form well-defined layers in the jar.

3 Fill the jar with layers of petals, pressing each layer down firmly with the pestle before you start the next. Add a few drops of an essential oil to enhance the fragrance, then replace the lid. Tie a ribbon around the neck of the jar.

Soap Giftboxes

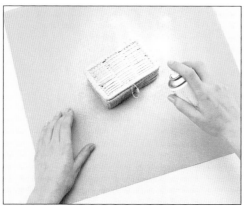

1 Spray a small wicker box lightly with white aerosol paint and allow to dry.

2 Wrap ribbon around the sides and base of the box and secure with adhesive tape. Tie another piece around the lid and finish with a bow on top. Stick a few shells on top of the bow using a strong, clear adhesive.

3 Half fill the box with shredded wood or tissue paper. Add a selection of shells, soaps, and bubblebath sachets with a seaside theme.

Celebration Crackers

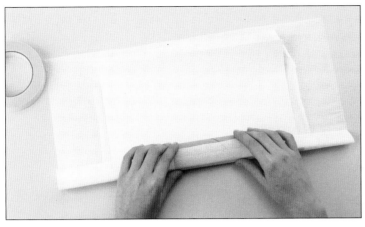

1 Lay a sheet of crêpe paper 10x14in (25x35cm) on a work surface and place a sheet of tissue 10x13in (25x32cm) on top. Place a piece of stiff paper 10x12in (25x30cm) on top of this, then a 4in (10cm) piece of cardboard tube in the center. Roll the layers up together and stick.

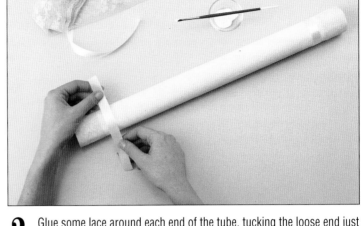

2 Glue some lace around each end of the tube, tucking the loose end just inside the free edge of crêpe paper at the back of the cracker. Glue a 1/2in (1cm) wide piece of ribbon around the tube about 1/2in (1cm) in from the piece of lace at each end.

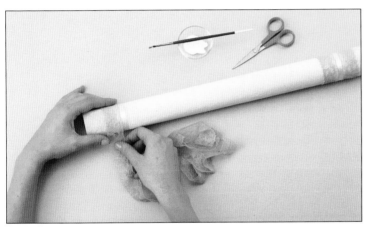

3 Take some narrow lace ribbon with a decorative edge and glue a piece on each side of the ribbon at either end of the tube. Tuck the loose ends inside the edge of the crêpe paper as before.

4 Slip a gift inside the cracker if desired (these crackers are nice enough to be used merely as keepsakes for your guests, so you don't have to add a gift) then gather each end up and tie firmly with nylon cord. Tie a lace bow around each piece of cord to cover.

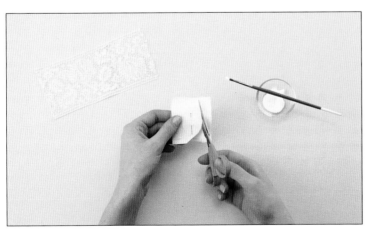

5 To make the cameo center, iron some adhesive backing onto a small piece of silk. Cut out a cameo shape, remove the backing and iron the silk onto a piece of wide lace ribbon.

6 Glue a piece of fine lace ribbon around the silk to cover the rough edges and embroider an initial or a name on the silk if you wish. Place the cameo in the center of the cracker and lightly glue the lace in place around the cracker.

Fabric Candy Parcels

1 Choose a fabric or selection of fabrics to fit in with your color scheme. Lay a dinner plate on the back of a piece of fabric and draw around it. Cut out the circle with pinking shears.

2 Choose a selection of candies such as chocolates or mints for your guests to eat after the meal. Lay on the fabric and bring the edges up around the candies.

3 Tie the parcels with ribbon or fabric tape to secure the tops. These parcels can be placed on side plates before the meal or just on the table next to each setting.

Miniature Topiaries

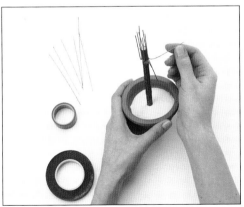

1 Secure the base of a twig in a terracotta pot with plaster of Paris. Take some short pieces of florist's wire and tape them, around their middles, to the top of the twig. Bend up the bottom halves of the wires so they are sticking straight up.

2 Take a small oasis ball and cover with dried moss, holding the pieces in place with staples made from short pieces of wire. When the ball is covered, trim off any loose moss, then press the ball firmly onto the spikes on top of the twig.

3 Insert small sprigs of dried gypsophila and alchemilla all over the surface of the ball to make a soft base. Add a few dried miniature roses and delphinium flowers for color. Finally, cover the surface of the pot with bun moss.

Tissue Paper Rose Bouquets

1 Cut a piece of tissue paper 10x5in (25x12cm). Fold over one third down the length. With the fold away from you, tuck in the top left corner then roll up the tissue paper to make a rose. Tuck in the top corner and twist the stem to finish.

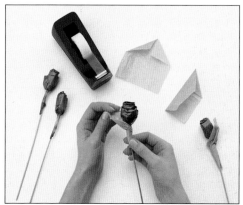

2 Stick a wooden skewer to the stem and cover the join with tissue paper. Repeat with as many roses as required. Make leaves from small squares of tissue. Fold down the top corners, fold in half down the length and attach to the stems.

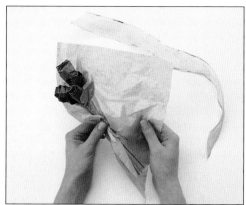

3 Arrange the roses into a posy and tie the stems together. Lay on a sheet of tissue paper and wrap it around them as you would wrap a bouquet. Wrap a ribbon around the stems and finish with a bow.

Pressed Flower Placecard

1 Make the placecard from a sheet of handmade paper. To tear handmade paper, mark out the placecard in pencil, then wet the paper along the line using a paintbrush. Leave to soak then carefully tear the paper along the moist line.

2 Fold the card in half and check that it stands up. Arrange pressed flowers on the front of the card along the bottom and up the right-hand side; add a small motif in the top left corner for balance. Choose a single flower for the back.

3 When you are happy with your design, stick the flowers in place using thinned glue applied in dots on the back of each flower with a wooden skewer. Allow the glue to dry, then write the name of the guest in the space provided.

Découpage Placecards

1 Cut out a series of motifs from magazines, greeting cards, or giftwrapping paper. We have chosen cherubs and flowers. Cut a piece of card 4x5in (10x12cm) and spray gold with aerosol paint. Fold in half when dry.

2 Score lightly along the fold with a craft knife. Arrange the cherub and flowers on the card and glue in place, making sure the cherub's head protrudes above the fold in the card.

3 Using a sharp craft knife, cut around the head of the cherub as far as the fold line on both sides. Now fold the card in half and the cherub's head will stand proud of the fold.

Velvet Napkin Ring

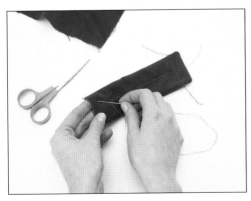

1 Cut two rectangles of velvet 3x8in (8x20cm). With right sides facing, sew three sides leaving a short end open; turn through. Sew across the width of the fabric ½in (1cm) from the closed end. Sew from the first seam along the center of the fabric to within 1in (2cm) of the open end.

2 You should now have two long pockets in the fabric. Stuff with lengths of cylindrical foam, pushing the foam in place with the blunt end of a pencil and working until the two sides are even. Sew across the width enclosing the foam, then turn in the raw edges and slipstitch the open end.

3 Using a rivet gun, make three rivet holes in each end of the napkin ring through the unpadded section. Thread cord through the holes and lace up as you would a shoe. Tie the cord in a neat knot or bow and slip a rolled napkin through the ring.

Harvest Posy

1 Arrange some ears of wheat into a neat bunch and add a few dried flowers to complete the posy. Wire the stems together tightly to hold firmly in place.

2 Braid three pieces of raffia, finishing the ends with knots as shown. Leave the loose, unbraided ends long.

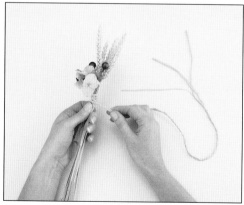

3 Tie one end of the raffia braid to the posy stems. Then wrap the braid around and around the stems to cover the wire. Finish by tying the loose ends of the raffia into a small bow. Trim the stems of the posy.

Christmas Gift Baskets

1 Wrap a piece of narrow plaid ribbon around and around the handle of a small basket and secure each end with adhesive tape or glue. Attach a sprig of artificial hollyberries to the base of the handle on either side.

2 Lightly spray four small pinecones and a few artificial leaves with gold paint. Attach wires to the bases of the cones and use the wires to fix the cones, two on each side, to the basket handle. Attach the artificial leaves in the same way.

3 Finish by tying a ribbon bow at each end of the handle, ensuring all the wires are covered. Fill the baskets with little Christmas gifts or with candies for your guests to eat after the meal.

Tussie Mussies

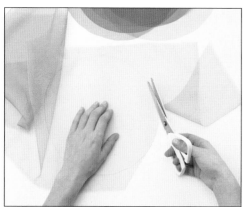

1 Using a dinner plate as a template, cut out four circles of sheer fabric for each tussie mussie, using a mixture of colors or just one color for each.

2 Choose a selection of flowers to complement the fabrics you have picked. Make little bouquets of flowers and foliage and wire the stems together to hold in place. Trim the stems to size, then cover the stems with green florist's tape.

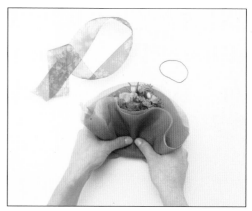

3 Lay four circles of fabric on a work surface and place a posy on top with the ends of the stems in the center of the fabric. Bring the fabric up around the flowers and secure around the stems with an elastic band. Cover with a ribbon.

Valentine Giftbox

1 Cut some long strips of tissue paper and crunch up in your hand. Draw two small hearts on corrugated paper and cut them out. Finally, make three tiny tissue paper roses (see page 60 for instructions).

2 Paint glue all over the top of the box lid. Starting from the outside edges, lay strips of crunched tissue on the glued surface to cover it completely. Stick the paper hearts and roses on top and finish with curled paper ribbon.

3 Allow the glue to dry thoroughly, then spray the outside of the box and the lid with gold paint. Allow the paint to dry. Then fill the box with shredded tissue paper and a gift.

PART TWO

NAPKIN FOLDING

Introduction

Decorative designs

Informal designs

Formal designs

INTRODUCTION

The Bow Tie's wavy effect is surprisingly easy to
achieve and looks most effective when displayed
on a decorative plate. Here, a silver napkin ring
complements a sea-green, linen napkin.

The use of table linen can be traced back to the Middle Ages when it
was fashionable to cover the table with a linen cloth and, by the end
of the 16th century, the wealthy classes had begun to sit down to
huge feasts at a more formal, 'laid' table. However, at this time,
people still ate with their fingers and, naturally, the ends of the
tablecloths (along with pieces of bread) were brought into use for
wiping greasy fingers and mouths. It was not unusual for a tablecloth
to be changed several times during the course of a meal and, when
laid diagonally, the corners of the cloth were even tucked into collars!
The natural progression was to tablecloths with removable linen
borders, eliminating the need to change the whole cloth.
The 17th century saw the introduction of forks and the penchant for
lavish meals. It was at this time that the first type of napkin was
used – initially a vast piece of linen, long enough to cover
the flamboyant clothing worn by both gentlemen and ladies of
the time, tied at the neck.

Decorative, folded napkins were introduced in the extravagant
Baroque era, and there were some quite extraordinary examples.
Napkins were folded to resemble birds, flowers and fans and, on
particularly splendid occasions, a different creation might be provided
for each guest. These ornate table decorations, some of them
permanently cut and sewn into place, were often kept from one meal
to the next with only the more simply folded ones actually being
used. At the turn of the 19th century many of the more intricate folds
remained in use, although these were generally kept for the ladies,
a simpler fold being used for the gentlemen.
Today, we are more likely to see folded linen napkins in restaurants
than in the home. However, with the use of attractive napkin rings
and bands, there is no reason why a stylish napkin should not be a
part of every well set table for any meal of the day. The more
elaborate designs are sure to create a memorable impression at a
dinner party or special celebration.

Basic Folding Tips

Creating a beautiful folded napkin is easy to do and there are only a few simple rules to follow and understand before successfully completing most of the folds in this book.

Firstly, ensure that hands and work surfaces are clean and always begin with an open napkin, placing it flat on the table in front of you. Try to fold on a cloth, as this will help the finished fold stand up.

When folding the napkin, always follow the directions carefully, bearing the following points in mind. If the directions tell you to fold 'down' into a rectangle or other shape, you should simply lift the edge of the napkin farthest away from you and fold it 'down' to meet the edge closest to you; do the opposite if you are instructed to fold 'up'.

The 'top edge' is the edge of the napkin farthest away from you;

similarly, the 'top point' refers to the angle farthest away from you. Sizes of napkins vary a good deal, but it is recommended that you don't use napkins less than 17 inches square. Napkins that are at least 20 inches square usually produce the best results and a dinner napkin, usually 26 inches square, is the ideal size to begin working with.

Cotton or linen napkins give the most elegant look and they fold best if freshly laundered, lightly starched and pressed. Napkins should be ironed flat and square at the corners. For the real perfectionist, napkins should be given a good soaking in cold-water starch and then mangled cold to obtain a stiff and dazzling quality. However, for the less committed, a can of spray starch gives very satisfactory

The Candle Fan looks dramatic unadorned, or you could add artificial flowers to soften the effect.

results, providing you do not use too much, or you may scorch the linen. Treated correctly, pure linen looks rich, takes folds well and is ideal for the more formal designs, while a cotton blend has a softer feel and lends itself well to more informal folds.

If you are fortunate enough to have lace napkins with decorative edges or embroidery, use folds that will show off their particular features. Many people like the look of delicate lace over a colored napkin; the two can be folded together for that extra special look.

If you prefer, all the designs in the book can be executed using paper napkins, usually available in cocktail and dinner sizes. Always buy the larger size and opt for the high-quality, thick type. If you can only obtain the cheaper, thinner variety, fold two or even three napkins together. Paper napkins can be suitable for even the most lavish of dinner parties when given the 'all star' treatment with elegant folding and the addition of a fresh flower or pretty ribbon.

Solid color napkins are usually best to work with, as those with a design printed on only one side have to be carefully folded to ensure that the printed side faces outward on the finished design.

It is both fun and practical to have a variety of napkins of different patterns, colors and materials. Though you may not be fortunate enough to inherit lovely linen, your napkins will far outlast any piece of crystal or china. Generally, most spills and stains can be easily removed.

For that special event, it is worthwhile putting a bit of extra thought into the presentation of your napkin. Stenciled decoration can be applied with stylish results and thoughtfully planned designs can complement your crockery, your cutlery or even the food itself. A stenciled Chinese motif, for example, would help to make an Oriental meal really memorable. For special events and celebration meals, the napkins are always more than protection for diners' clothing – they are there to enhance and enliven even the most minimal table setting.

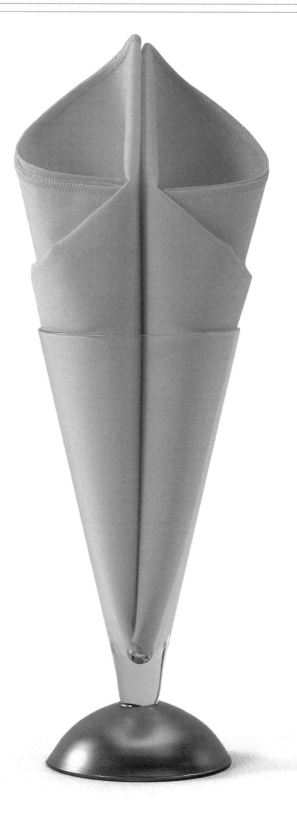

Above: Shown off particularly well in a conical glass, the Double Cornet makes a handsome display.

Left: You can make this pretty napkin ring by simply threading colorful beads on to thin elastic cord.

CHAPTER FOUR

DECORATIVE DESIGNS

For special celebrations it's worth taking a little extra time to make up stylish
and unusual napkin designs. Bits and pieces around the house can come in
useful for creating imaginative table settings that everyone will remember.

Copy-cat Napkin Ring

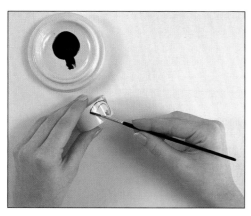

1 Decorate some napkin rings to match your plates. You will need ceramic paints that match the colors of your china: in this case blue, green and pink. First, paint the outline of the design using a very fine brush and being careful to make a single sweeping movement with each stroke.

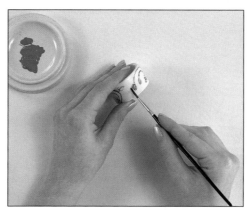

2 When the initial coat is dry, begin to fill in the outline with a second color, carefully following the design on your plate.

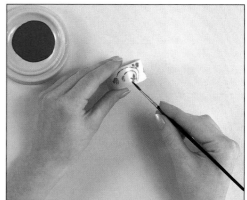

3 Finish off with a third and, if necessary, a fourth color, allowing each coat to dry before applying a new one. Protect the design with a coat of ceramic varnish. If you wish to decorate your table napkins too, follow the same procedure using fabric paints.

Lacy Napkin Folder

1 Here's a quick and simple way to dress up a plain napkin for an afternoon tea party. All you need is a square paper doily, slightly larger than the napkin and preferably in a contrasting color, and a floral motif. Begin by folding the napkin into a triangle.

2 Fold the doily diagonally. To create a 'spine' to allow for the thickness of the napkin, unfold the doily and make another crease about 3/8 inch below the first fold.

3 Cut out a floral motif such as a Victorian scrap and glue it to the center of the smaller (top) side of the doily. Insert the napkin.

Thanksgiving Napkin

1 This simple place setting is perfect for a Thanksgiving dinner. Use a sisal or straw placemat and a plain white napkin. For the decoration you will need a selection of dried flowers and grasses, and three lengths of beige ribbon, each about 20 inches long.

2 Tie the lengths of ribbon together at one end. Braid them until the braid is long enough to wrap around the napkin twice with a little left over to tie underneath.

3 Group the bunch of dried flowers and grasses together, securing them with thread or twine. Fold the napkin in half twice to form a long, narrow rectangle. Lay the flowers on top of the napkin. Wind the braided ribbon around the napkin and flowers twice and tie the ends under the napkin.

Lacy Napkin Bow

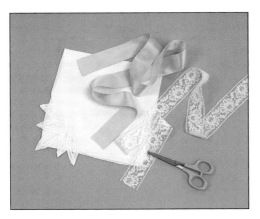

1 Ideal for a wedding or anniversary dinner, this lacy napkin bow is not only pretty but also easy to make. The napkins themselves should preferably have a lace detail around the edge. For each napkin you will need about 1 yard of wide satin ribbon and the same amount of insertion lace.

2 For the best results, the napkin should be starched and well ironed, and folded into quarters. To cut decorative points for the ribbon and lace, fold the ends as shown and cut them diagonally.

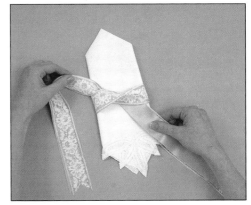

3 Fold under two corners of the napkin to overlap in the center, forming the shape shown here. Iron the folds flat. Lay the ribbon and lace flat, wrong side up, with the ribbon on top. Place the napkin on top and tie the ribbon and lace around it in a bow.

Festive Napkin Rings

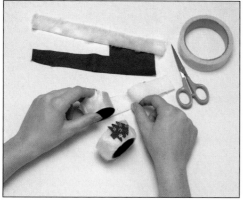

1 Make some especially festive napkin rings for Christmas. Each one is made from a piece of cardboard tubing. Stick a strip of fake fur to the outside, to represent snow, and green felt to disguise the cardboard on the inside. Top it with a tiny green felt Christmas tree sparkling with sequins.

2 The leaf sprig ring is first covered with a strip of gummy-backed plastic. Cut the plastic wide enough to go over to the inside of the ring, and cover the inside with a thinner strip of ribbon. The leaf design with a red bow is a Christmas cake decoration.

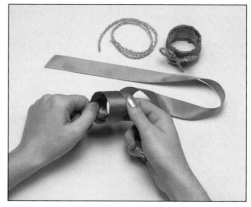

3 Still another idea is to cover the ring with a small strip of wide satin ribbon. Glue a piece of narrower toning ribbon to the inside, folding the edges of the wide ribbon under as you go. Lastly, tie a strand of tinsel wire around the ring and finish with a bow.

Tassel Napkin Ring

1 This tasseled napkin ring is ideal for a special occasion. You will need two tassels and about 16 inches of cord per napkin, and a strong fabric glue. Attach the tassels to the cord by wrapping the loop around the cord and pulling the tassel through it.

2 Make the ring by feeding the cord through both loops of the tassels twice more. Make sure that the ring is large enough to slip easily over the napkin.

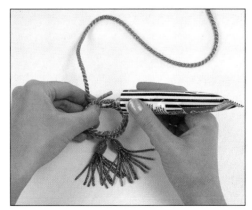

3 Using a strong glue, secure the ends of the cord to the back of the ring. Lay one end along the back and trim it. Having applied the glue to the inside of the ring as shown, wrap the remaining end over the cords, covering the trimmed end. Cut the remaining cord on the inside, and clamp in place until dry.

Floral Napkin Ring

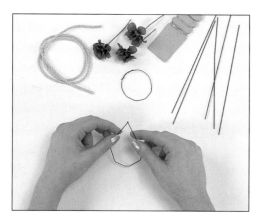

1 This charming flower-trimmed napkin ring adds a touch of elegance to a table setting and is very easy to make. Bend a short length of florists' wire into a circle and twist the ends together to secure them.

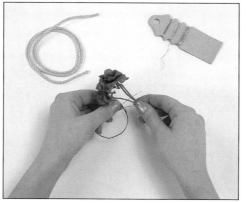

2 Wind some very fine wire around one or two small silk flowers – chosen to co-ordinate with your china and table linen. Then twist the ends of the wire around the circle of florists' wire to hold the flowers in place.

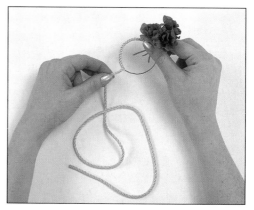

3 Use narrow decorative braid to cover the wire. Hold one end in place with one hand, and use the other hand to twist the braid around the circle to cover it, beginning and ending underneath the flowers. Secure the ends with glue. Insert the napkin and add a fresh flower.

Stenciled Shell Napkin

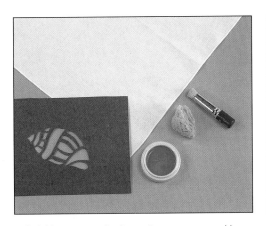

1 You can easily decorate your own napkins with a stencil design to complement your china or decorative scheme. All you need is a plain napkin or a hemmed square of fabric, a stencil motif (either bought or original), a natural sponge and some fabric paint.

2 Position the stencil on the napkin. Mix the paint in a saucer. Dip the sponge into the paint and dab it on a piece of scrap paper to remove the excess. Alternatively, you can use a stencil brush, which will give a slightly different effect from a sponge.

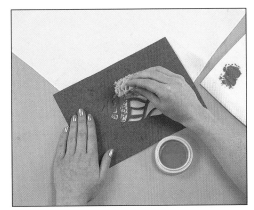

3 You can either hold the stencil in place with your fingers or fasten it with tape. Dab paint through the stencil onto the fabric, taking care that it doesn't seep under the edges. When the paint is dry, fix it following the manufacturer's directions.

Golden Leaves

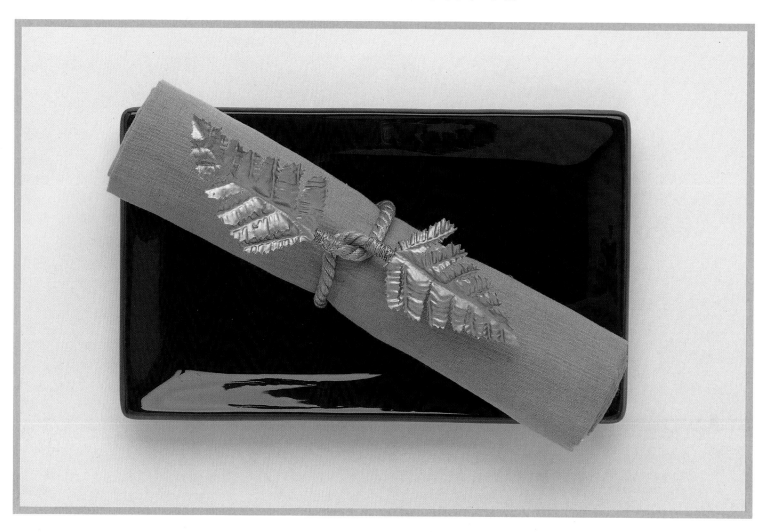

1 This is a very stylish napkin idea and is ideal for a special dinner party. You will need enough florists' wire to wrap around each napkin one and a half times. Paint or spray silk fern leaves gold, allowing two leaves for each napkin. Leave to dry completely.

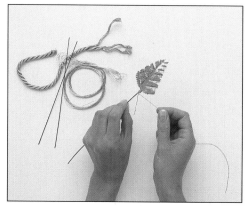

2 Twist the ends of the wire around the stems of the fern leaves, securing them tightly, so that they can be curved easily.

3 Cover the wire completely using fine gold braid or ribbon. Twist tightly so the braid will not unravel and stick it down at regular intervals with glue. Twist the wire loosely around a rolled napkin with the leaves uppermost.

Stiffened Bow

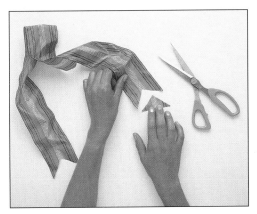

1 This attractive napkin ring will add instant charm to any table setting. You will need a 36 inch ribbon for each napkin. Choose a ribbon to match your china. Cut the ends of the ribbon into points by folding them double and cutting a diagonal across the fold.

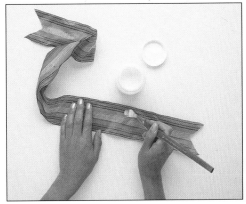

2 Coat both sides of the ribbon with fabric glue and tie a bow loosely around a glass bottle that has a diameter similar to that of the napkin roll. Leave until almost dry.

3 Slide the ring off the bottle and leave until completely dry. Insert a napkin that has been loosely rolled.

Ballerina

1 This is a pretty decoration for a little girl's birthday party and the clothespin dolls can be taken home afterwards. You will need the old-fashioned type of clothespin and non-toxic water-based paint. Each doll will need one pipe cleaner for her arms.

2 Pleat two small paper napkins into 'accordion' folds and fold each napkin in half. Construct the doll using the main photograph for reference.

3 Wrap two napkin skirts around each doll and tie them on securely with thread or fine ribbon. Finally, fan out the folds to give the effect of a ballerina's skirt.

Beaded Napkin Ring

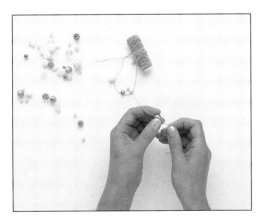

1 This napkin ring uses those broken necklaces and loose beads and looks rather like a miniature bracelet.

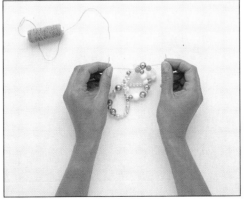

2 Use thin elastic to thread the beads and knot the ends together securely. The rings should be big enough to slip easily over a rolled napkin. Make as many strands of beads as you like and secure the rings together by knotting across the width at regular intervals.

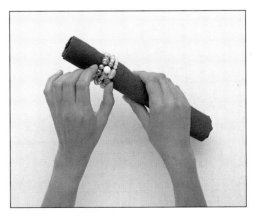

3 A dark-colored napkin shows off this beaded ring most effectively. Roll up the napkin neatly and insert into the ring.

Decorated Napkins

1 For the blue napkins, cut a star shape from a piece of cardboard – the cardboard must be slightly wider than the folded napkin. Hold the cardboard firmly in place over each napkin and spray gold or silver paint over the area. Let the paint dry for several minutes before you allow anything else to touch it.

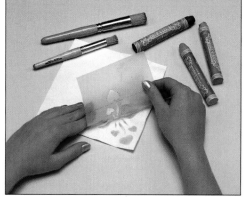

2 A purchased stencil and oil-based stencil crayons are used for the decoration on the white napkins. Place your chosen design over the area you want to stencil. Rub the crayon over a spare area of stencil, then take the color up onto the brush and paint it over the stencil, in a circular motion.

3 Use the brush only over the parts you wish to show up in that color. Then switch to the next color. It is best to use a different brush for each color if you want a clear color definition.

Plaid Napkin

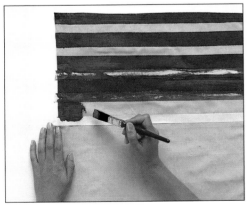

1 Use only three colors of fabric paint and decorate plain napkins to produce some stunning designs. Paint wide horizontal bands across a plain napkin, either freehand or using masking tape to ensure neater edges. If you prefer, make a paper pattern first to show the positions of the bands.

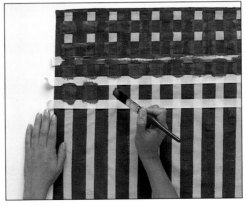

2 Paint vertical bands of the same width as the horizontal ones from top to bottom of the napkin, using another color.

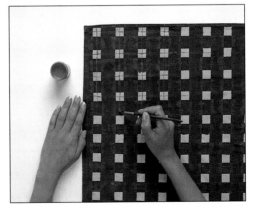

3 Use a smaller brush and a third color to paint a fine stripe between the bands horizontally and vertically to complete the plaid napkin. When dry, fold the napkin as liked.

Ribboned Napkin Ring

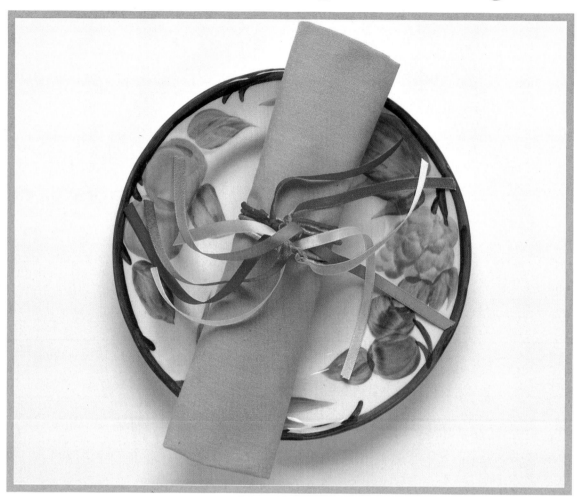

1 This attractive napkin ring makes use of various lengths of ribbon that might otherwise be thrown away. Measure the circumference of a napkin ring and cut a pipe cleaner to this size. Wrap a length of ribbon tightly around the pipe cleaner, leaving a piece of ribbon free at each end. Secure the ribbon with thread.

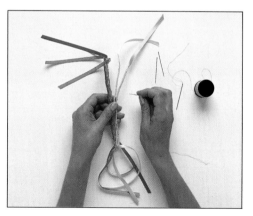

2 Cover four or five matching lengths of pipe cleaner in the same way, using different colors of ribbon. Then sew each length together carefully to make a multi-colored band.

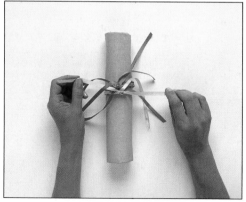

3 Shape the band round to form a ring and insert a napkin. Tie each ribbon securely, allowing the ends to curl as shown.

Jeweled Napkin Ring

1 This napkin ring will add sparkle to any table setting for a special occasion. You will need a small block of air-drying modeling clay, available at most art and craft stores. Roll out the clay and form it into a ring. A crown shape is shown in the photograph but you can sculpt any design you wish.

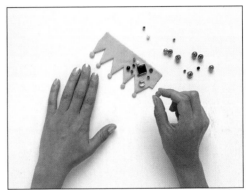

2 While the clay is still soft, press a selection of multi-colored gems or beads into the ring and leave to dry.

3 Paint the bare parts of the ring decoratively, taking care not to touch the gems or beads, and leave to dry. Brush the ring with acrylic varnish to protect it.

Net Napkin Ring

1 For a touch of frivolity, tie your table napkins in several shades of net. For each napkin cut three rectangles of different-colored net, 19 x 13 inch. Fold each piece crosswise into three equal sections.

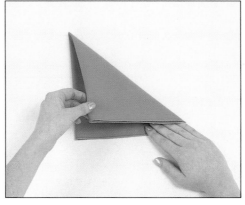

2 Fold the napkin twice to form a square, and then fold it diagonally to form a triangle. Then roll it lengthwise.

3 Place the pieces of net on top of each other; tie them around the napkin and fan out the ends.

CHAPTER FIVE

INFORMAL DESIGNS

Colorful and patterned napkins are ideal for informal designs – you
can even cut squares from fabric remnants (simply sew a hem around the
edges) or use paper napkins. With a little flair you can enliven a table
setting for any occasion.

Gingerbread Man Envelope

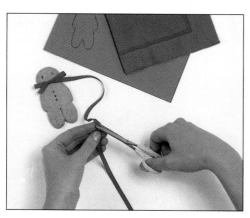

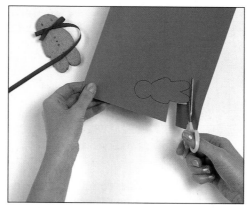

1 Sure to be a hit with children, each little gingerbread man is tucked into a napkin and has his own place card 'shadow'. Copy the shape of the gingerbread man onto stiff colored paper; set it aside. Using a length of narrow satin ribbon, tie a bow around the neck of the gingerbread man, leaving an end about 6 inches long to be attached to the place card.

2 Cut the ends of the ribbon into points by folding them double and cutting a diagonal across the fold. Cut the drawn shape from the colored paper.

3 Write the child's name on the shape. Apply a dab of glue and stick the card shape onto the ribbon. Fold back one corner of a bright-colored paper napkin to make an envelope for the gingerbread man.

The Triangle Pouch

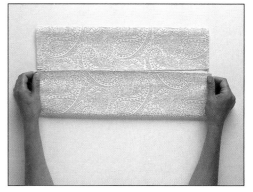

1 The prepared napkins can be piled on top of each other or fanned out into a circle for a buffet meal. Fold the left- and right-hand edges inwards to meet in the center. Fold the top edge down to make a narrow rectangle.

2 Press the top right-hand corner and fold the bottom right-hand corner up slightly so it now touches an imaginary horizontal line.

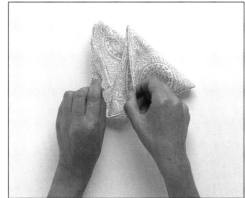

3 Place a finger on the bottom right-hand corner and fold the top right-hand corner down to meet the bottom edge. Repeat the fold and tuck the last flap inside to form the pouch.

The Ruffle

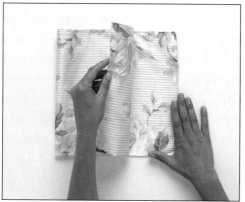

1 Floral chintz napkins with this pretty fold are perfect for a summer tea party or luncheon outside. Fold the napkin in half left to right and in half again top to bottom. Place in front of you with the open corners pointing upwards.

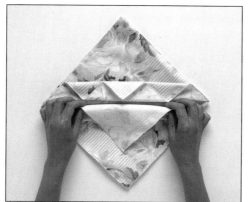

2 Fold the first layer down and pleat it four times. Repeat with the second layer, placing this above the first layer of pleats. Press.

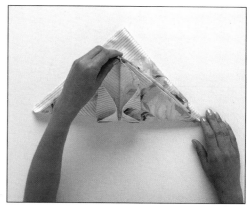

3 Turn the napkin so the pleats are vertical. Fold the napkin in half with the pleats on the outside and arrange on a plate.

Everyday Fold

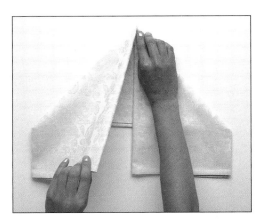

1 This looks pretty on the breakfast, lunch or dinner table, with toast or a bread roll kept warm inside the pouch. Start by folding the napkin into three, then fold down the left- and right-hand edges as shown.

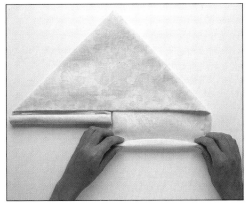

2 Turn the napkin over and roll up the two overhanging edges tightly to the base of the triangle. Fold across the center so that the rolled edges are on the outside.

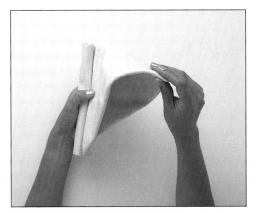

3 Hold the napkin by the rolled section and squash the farthest part of the triangle across the diagonal and open out the napkin. Place on a plate.

Breakfast Fold

1 Let the children paint a section of a cardboard tube for the napkin ring and display the prepared napkin on a breakfast tray. Fold the four corners into the center and fold in half left to right and in half again bottom to top to make a small square.

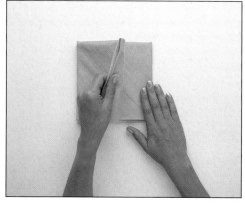

2 Fold the top layer of the right-hand corner down and fold back the top left- and bottom right-hand corners, tucking them in neatly behind the napkin.

3 Press the sides back and slip the napkin through the ring until the lower flap just covers the top of the ring.

Envelope

1 Always popular with children, any number of treats can be hidden within the folds of this napkin. Adults might prefer a flower as shown in the main photograph! Fold the napkin in half across the diagonal, then fold the two outside edges into thirds along the lower edge.

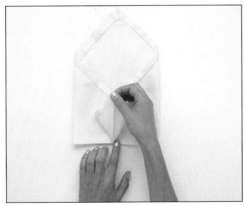

2 Place a finger over the center of the napkin across all thicknesses and fold back the right-hand flap across the center, squashing down the triangular flap to make a small diamond shape as shown.

3 Fold down the top point of the napkin and tuck it into the diamond shape to close the envelope. Insert a flower if wished.

Bow Tie

1 This pretty fold is both simple and effective. Start by folding the napkin in half from left to right and in half again from top to bottom to form a square. Place the napkin in front of you with the open points to the left.

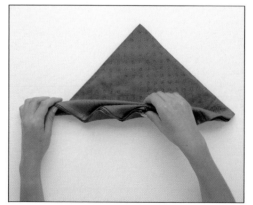

2 Starting at the bottom, pleat the napkin with 'accordion' folds of equal depth to form a strip that will fit into the ring.

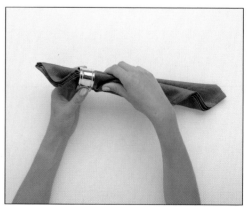

3 Slip the napkin through the ring to the center and arrange the folds into a fan shape, as shown in the main photograph.

Oriental Fold

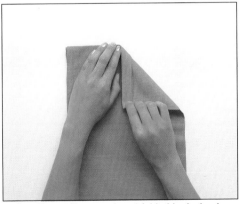

1 Almost like an origami fold, this design is simple to achieve and looks very stylish. Fold the napkin in half left to right and fold the top edge behind by only 1 inch. Place a finger at the center of the top edge and fold the left- and right-hand corners to meet in the center and form a triangle.

2 Fold up the bottom edge by only 1 inch to the front of the napkin and fold over the same edge to overlap the base of the triangle by 1 inch.

3 Hold a finger at the center point of this flap and fold together the left- and right-hand corners to form a second triangle. Fold behind the right- and left-hand edges to create a neat shape.

Circular Napkin

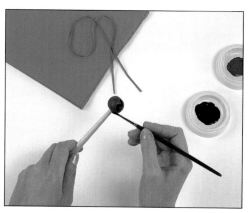

1 This original napkin fold has a bead and ribbon trimming. Paint a plain 1 inch wooden bead with a water-based paint to match your napkin. Allow to dry. Then paint on a pattern in a harmonizing or contrasting color.

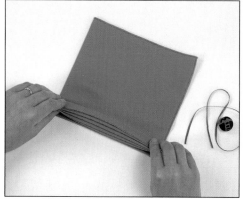

2 Fold the napkin in half once along its length, and then pleat it accordion-style along its length, making sure that the folds are all exactly the same size.

3 Thread a length of narrow ribbon through the bead and tie it to hold the bead in place. Wrap the ribbon around the center of the napkin and tie it in a neat bow just below the bead. Fan the napkin out so that it forms a full circle.

The Sailing Boat

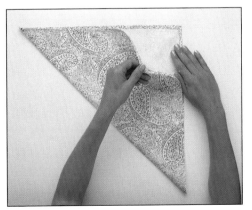

1 A smaller napkin may be used for this fold and it works equally well with linen or paper. Start by folding the napkin in half diagonally.

2 With the base of the triangle nearest you, roll the base up towards the top of the triangle. Roll as tightly as you can and stop rolling approximately 2½ inches from the top point.

3 Fold the napkin in half with the rolled edge inwards and arrange the boat on a plate with the edge extending over the rim.

The Waves

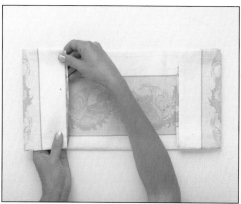

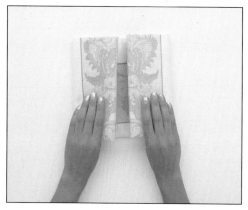

1 A simple fold that can be used at any time. Start by folding the napkin into three so you have a long narrow rectangle. Fold the left- and right-hand edges inwards, folding over twice on each side so that the edges meet in the center.

2 Turn the napkin over and fold in half from side to side. Then turn the napkin over again to reveal the 'waves'.

3 Slightly spread the three 'waves' apart. Small flower heads or menu cards can be tucked into the folds.

The Pineapple

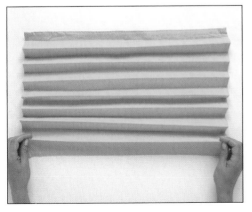

1 A very simple, frilly fold which benefits from the addition of a pretty napkin ring. Start by pleating the napkin from top to bottom, accordion-style, making sure that the pleats are all the same size.

2 Holding the edges tightly, fold the napkin in half. Pull about two-thirds of the folded edge through the napkin ring as shown.

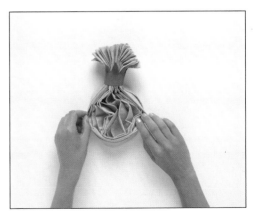

3 Push the ring over the napkin to within 2 inches of the open ends. Pull out the top folds to create the spiky leaves and plump out the base to make a nice fat pineapple shape.

Peacock's Tail

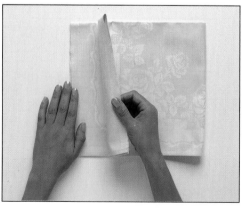

1 This design resembles the fan of a peacock's tail. Fold a square napkin in half from top to bottom so that the fold is at the top. Fold the right-hand edge over to meet the left-hand one as shown.

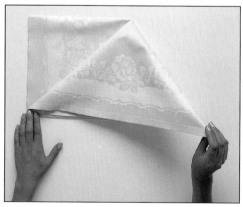

2 Keeping a finger on the center of the bottom layer, pull over the top layer of the bottom left-hand corner to form a triangle.

3 Turn the napkin over and pull over the top layer of the bottom right-hand corner to form a triangle. Fold the triangle in half and fan out the four points that have formed underneath, spacing them evenly. Place on a plate with the points facing upwards.

CHAPTER SIX

FORMAL DESIGNS

Impress your guests with a fabulous table display featuring formal napkin designs, ensuring that your meal has the best possible start. Most formal designs work well when made up with large napkins – choose the finest linen for intricate folds.

Lotus Blossom

1 This pretty design is not as difficult to create as it may appear. The technique is similar to that used in folding the origami 'fortune cookies' so popular with children. Lay the napkin flat, and begin by folding each of the four corners into the center.

2 Repeat this procedure, turning the corners inwards to make an even smaller square. Then turn the napkin over and repeat for a third time, holding the corners down in the center to keep them in place.

3 Still keeping your fingers on the center, reach under the napkin with your other hand to one of the corners and draw this outwards gently until it peaks out. Repeat with the other corners to form the petals. Draw out the four single-thickness flaps to make the sepals.

Pure and Simple

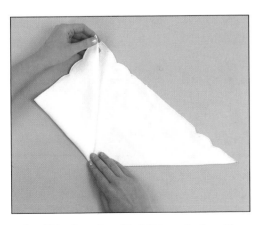

1 This elegant napkin fold is easier to achieve than it looks. An embroidered napkin with a scalloped edge is particularly suitable for this design. First fold the napkin in half diagonally, then bring the left- and right-hand corners up to meet at the apex, thus forming a square.

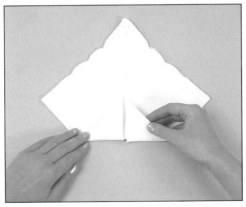

2 Turn the napkin over, and fold one corner up slightly as shown, taking care that the point is aligned with the apex.

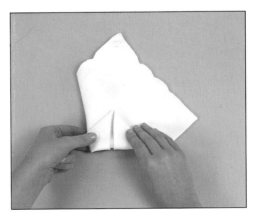

3 Fold the left- and right-hand corners underneath the napkin on a slight diagonal, pressing the folds lightly in place.

Double Jabot

1 Fold the napkin twice to form a square and position it with the free corners at the top right. Fold the top corner back diagonally to meet the lower left corner, then turn it back on itself as shown. Continue to fold the corner back and forth to create a 'accordion' effect along the diagonal strip of napkin.

2 Lift the next layer of fabric from the top right-hand corner and repeat the procedure described in the first step to create two parallel strips with zigzag edges.

3 Pick the napkin up in both hands with the zigzag folds in the center. Fold it in half diagonally to form a triangle, keeping the pleats on the inside. Hold the right- and left-hand corners of the triangle and curl them back, tucking one into the other to secure. Stand the napkin upright on a plate as shown.

Pure Elegance

1 For best results use a crisply starched napkin to make this attractive fold which is a good choice for an elegant dinner party. First fold the napkin lengthwise into three to form a long rectangle. Lay it horizontally with the free edge away from you, and fold the left- and right-hand ends inwards to meet at the center.

2 Fold down the top right- and left-hand corners to meet in the center, forming a point. Hold the napkin in both hands and flip it over towards you so that the point is facing you and the flat side of the napkin is uppermost.

3 Lift the sides and pull them over towards one another to form a cone shape. Tuck the left-hand corner into the right-hand corner to secure it. Turn the napkin around and place it on a plate as shown in the photograph.

The Princess

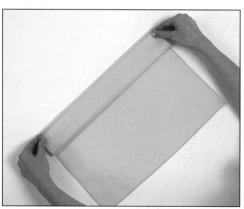

1 Fold the napkin in half to form a crease along the center line. Then open the napkin out. Fold one half of the napkin lengthwise into three by bringing the top edge of the square inwards to the center line and then folding it back on itself as shown. Repeat with the second half.

2 Fold the napkin in half lengthwise by tucking one half under the other along the center line. Lay the resulting strip flat with the three folded edges facing you. Mark the center of this strip with a finger and fold the right-hand edge in towards the center and back on itself as shown. Repeat on the left-hand side.

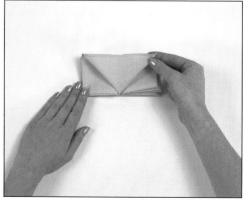

3 Pull the top left-hand corner across towards the top right-hand corner to make a triangle, pressing down gently along the folds to hold them in place. Repeat with the remaining left-hand folds, and then do the same with all the right-hand folds. Ease the folds open slightly and display the napkin as shown.

The Bishop's Hat

1 This miter-shaped fold can be displayed either on a flat surface or in a glass, cup or soup bowl, which allows the flaps to drape gracefully over the sides. Begin by folding the napkin diagonally to form a triangle, then pull each corner up to the apex as shown to make a square.

2 Turn the napkin over so that the free edges lie towards you. Pull the two top flaps up and away from you; then fold the remaining two flaps back in the same way to form a triangle.

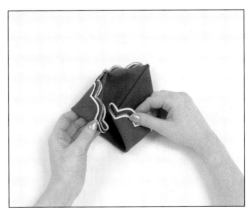

3 Turn the napkin over carefully, and pull the two outer corners together so that they overlap; tuck one flap into the folds of the other to hold them in place. Finally, turn the front of the 'hat' to face you, position the napkin upright and pull the loose flaps down to rest on the plate as shown in the main photograph.

Oriental Fan

1 This effective design benefits from a well-starched napkin. Fold the napkin in half lengthwise and then fold one end of the rectangle backwards and forwards in accordion-style folds, until just past the halfway point.

2 Holding the folds firmly together, fold the napkin lengthwise down the middle to bring both ends of the 'accordion' together. Keeping the folds in position in one hand, fold the loose flap of the napkin over across the diagonal.

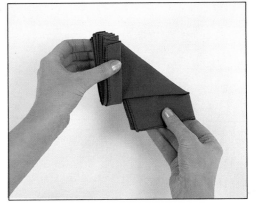

3 Push the flap underneath the support as shown to balance the napkin and, letting go of the pleats, allow the fan to fall gently into position.

Double Cornet

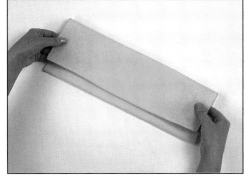

1 This design looks best in a conical glass but can be adapted for a wider-based container. Although it takes a little more practice than most, it is worth the effort. First lay the napkin flat and fold it in three lengthwise. Position it as shown, with the free edge on top.

2 Take hold of the top left- and right-hand corners of the napkin with the index finger and thumb of each hand. Roll the corners diagonally towards you as shown.

3 Still holding the napkin, continue to roll the corners inwards in one sweeping movement by swiveling both hands and napkin down, up and over until your hands are together palms uppermost. By now the napkin should be rolled into two adjacent flutes. Place the napkin in a glass, arranging it neatly.

Pocket Napkin

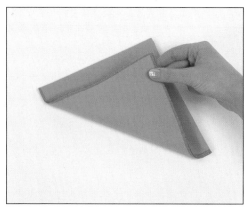

1 This simple napkin fold is embellished with a few artificial flowers tucked into the pocket. Fold the napkin in half and then in half again to form a square; then fold it across the diagonal to form a triangle.

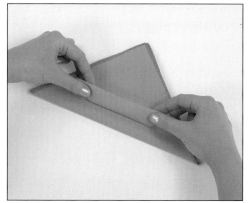

2 Position the napkin as shown with the four free corners uppermost. Working with the top layer only, fold it down several times to make a cuff at the bottom.

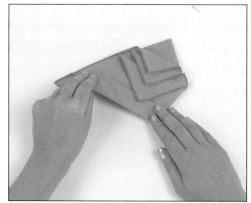

3 Fold the next (single) corner over so that the tip touches the top edge of the cuff. Fold the next two corners over to form three tiers. Then turn the right- and left-hand corners of the triangle to the underside and overlap them. Position the napkin as shown in the main photograph and insert the flowers in the top opening.

Lady's Slipper

1 This pretty design is ideally suited to tea-time settings. Begin by folding the napkin into four – left to right, top to bottom – for form a small square. Then fold the four free corners back across the diagonal to form a triangle.

2 Holding the napkin firmly at the apex, fold one of the outer corners over and towards you as shown, so that it overlaps the base of the triangle. Repeat with the second corner so that the edges of both flaps meet down the center of the napkin to form a kite shape.

3 Turn the napkin over and fold the protruding flaps back over the base of the triangle. Then fold the triangle in half by pulling one of the corners over to meet the other. Holding both corners firmly together, turn the napkin upright and pull the four free corners upwards as shown in the main photograph. Arrange on a plate.

Four Feathers

1 This simple fold looks elegant placed in a wine glass. Lay the napkin flat. Fold it in half to form a triangle, with the folded edge towards you. Place your index finger on the center of this edge. Using the top layer of fabric only, bring the apex down to meet the left-hand corner.

2 Again working with the top layer only, bring the far corner down and across to the bottom left-hand corner.

3 Bring the remaining top corner down and across to the lower left corner as before, forming a triangle. Splay the folds slightly, then turn the napkin over so that the folds are underneath. Lift the edge and roll the napkin into a loose cone shape, stopping about halfway across. Fold up the bottom point and place the napkin in a glass, preferably one with a thick stem.

Candle Fold

1 This tall candle-shaped fold looks especially good if the napkin has a contrasting border. Lay the napkin flat. Fold it in half diagonally to form a triangle. Turn up the folded edge about 1¼ inch, then turn the napkin over so that the fold is underneath.

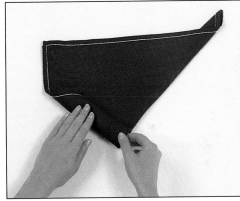

2 Beginning at the left-hand corner, roll the napkin carefully to form a cylindrical shape with the folded edge outwards.

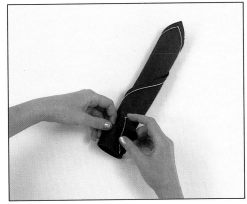

3 Tuck in the end to hold the roll in place. Finally, fold down the front corner at the top as shown in the main photograph.

Pointed Pleats

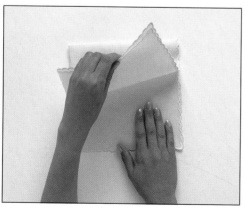

1 This fold works particularly well with napkins that have scalloped or embroidered edges. Fold the napkin in half left to right and in half again top to bottom. Place the napkin in front of you with the closed corners uppermost.

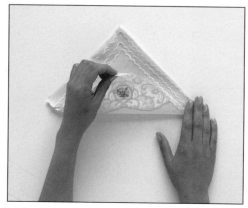

2 Bring the layers up in tiers to meet the top point, leaving an equal space between each layer as shown.

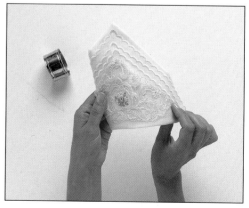

3 Fold the left- and right-hand sides behind the napkin and stand the pointed pleats in a napkin ring.

Lily

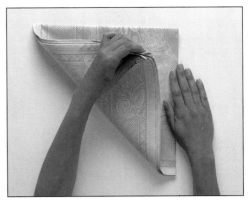

1 This is a quick and simple way to create a stunning table display with the napkins attractively displayed in wine glasses. Begin by folding the napkin into four left to right, top to bottom so you have a square. Fold in half across the diagonal to form a triangle.

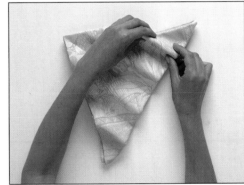

2 Turn the napkin so that the apex is away from you as shown. Starting at the bottom point, pleat from right to left.

3 Hold the base of the napkin firmly in one hand and insert in a wine glass keeping the pleats intact. Hold the top of the napkin and pull each individual pleat forward as shown to display the petals of the Lily.

Deco Fold

1 Spray a large dinner napkin with a little starch to hold the folds for this design. Fold the four corners to meet in the center, then fold in half left to right and in half again top to bottom to make a small square. Place the square in front of you so the points are facing down.

2 Bring the single top layer up to the top point leaving a gap of ½ inch at the top. Repeat with the three remaining layers, leaving an equal space between each layer.

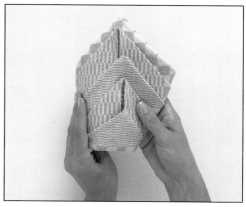

3 Fold back the left and right sides to create the final shape as shown and arrange on a plate with the base nearest you.

The Umbrella

1 A crisply starched napkin is required for this very attractive fold. Pleat the napkin into six equal 'accordion' folds.

2 Tuck each fold in on itself at right angles and carefully press flat each triangular pocket that has been formed.

3 Hold the bottom left- and right-hand corners and fold the napkin across so that the two held points meet in the center of the napkin. Open up the folds and arrange the pleats outwards. Place the napkin on a plate and lay a flower in the center, if desired.

Miter

1 This decorative fold originates from origami. Start by folding the napkin in half, keeping the open sides to the top. Fold up the bottom left-hand corner and fold down the top right-hand corner until they meet in the center.

2 Turn the napkin over and position the long edges at the top and bottom. Fold the napkin in half and fold up the right-hand point from underneath.

3 Tuck the left-hand point inside the right-hand flap. Turn the napkin over and tuck the right-hand point into the left-hand flap. Open out the fold a little and position on a plate.

Candle Fan

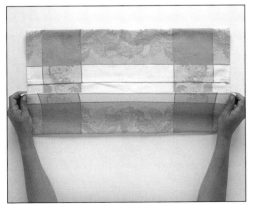

1 It is best to use a large white starched napkin for this elegant design which may be decorated with fresh or artificial flowers, or a sprig of holly at Christmas. Fold the left- and right-hand edges inwards to meet at the center.

2 Place a finger firmly on the center of the napkin to hold the edges together and fold each corner back diagonally.

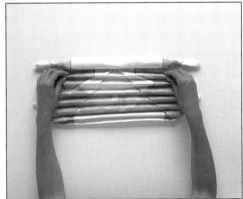

3 Tightly roll the top half of the napkin and pleat the lower half from bottom to top. Fold in half widthwise, place in a wine glass and gently pull out the folded pleats.

Palm Leaf

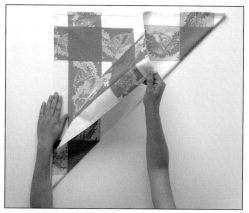

1 This stylish fold will benefit from a well starched napkin and the finest linen. Begin by folding the napkin in half diagonally.

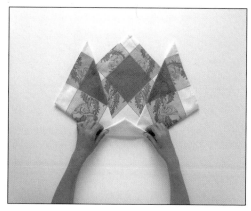

2 Fold the left- and right-hand corners towards the center, leaving a gap of 2 inches between the inside edges. Fold up a 2 inch hem from the base and pleat from left to right across the napkin.

3 Set the base of the fold in a napkin ring or glass and open out the folds to form the palm leaf.

The Guard of Honor

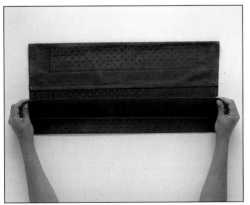

1 This impressive design will hold tighter rolls if the napkin has first been well starched. Begin by folding both sides towards the center until they meet.

2 Place a finger firmly on the center of the napkin and fold each corner back diagonally to form projecting triangles.

3 Tightly roll the edge nearest to you up towards the center of the napkin, then roll the farthest edge down to meet the other roll in the center. Put a hand in the middle of the rolls, bend the napkin up at each side and interlock the four points. Finish by placing a bread roll or flower in the middle of the fold.

The Fan

1 This is definitely the napkin to impress! Start with a large, well starched napkin and fold the lower edge up towards the top edge, leaving a space of 2 inches. Fold up the new lower edge, again leaving a space of 2 inches.

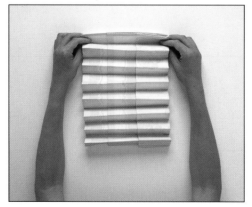

2 Pleat the napkin from left to right, accordion-style, pressing the folds firmly each time.

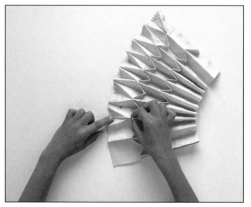

3 Hold the napkin at the base and pull forward the edges on the bottom row where the pleats have been folded backwards, to make tiny triangular pockets. Continue along all the pleats on the bottom row and repeat the same process on the middle row, pressing the pockets. On the top row, fold the forward-facing pleats to make similar triangular pockets, facing backwards. Close the fan and press. Open the fan and arrange as shown.

The Butterfly

1 A crisply starched napkin is required for this pretty fold. Lay the napkin flat. Fold two edges to meet in the center as shown. Then fold the half nearest you across the center line and over on the top of the other half, to form a long, narrow rectangle.

2 Fold the right-hand end of the rectangle in towards the center, and with another fold double it back on itself as shown. Repeat with the left-hand side so that the double folds meet in the center.

3 Pull the right-hand back corner across to the left, bringing the front edge across the center line to form a triangle. Holding the right-hand side with one hand, use the other hand to fold the corner back to its original position, thus creating the 'wings' of the butterfly. Repeat the procedure on the left-hand side so that the napkin has two symmetrical wings you can arrange to look like the completed fold, shown above.

PART THREE

GIFTWRAPPING

Introduction

130

Giftwrapping Papers

133

Boxes, Fabrics & Bags

149

Finishing Touches

171

INTRODUCTION

Everyday objects such as buttons can be used to add a personal touch to a gift in otherwise plain paper. Choose the buttons to complement the color of the paper and ribbon selected.

The giving of presents is always a very enjoyable and pleasing experience, and the more attractive a gift looks, the more the enjoyment is increased - for both the giver and the receiver. Unfortunately, it can sometimes seem that the wrapping is almost as expensive as the gift itself, so in this book you will find many ideas which are effective and easy to achieve with the minimum of cost, and in many cases with the minimum of time.

Today there are so many styles of giftwrapping paper available, that whatever the gift or occasion, it is likely you will find something to suit. However, why not personalize the wrapping by adding a handmade gift tag or enhance it with additional decoration? This book will give you a host of ideas on how to do just that. There are also ideas for creating your own paper designs, or using alternatives such as fabric, tissue or even tin foil. Whatever the gift, you will find the perfect solution to wrap, enhance and decorate it.

There are, of course, many other materials that can be used to wrap presents. Just look around the home or garden and you will find lots of ideas. For example, in Chapter Seven, there is a gift wrapped in sheet music, but another idea would be to wrap a child's gift in pages from a brightly-colored comic, with a matching tag and bright ribbon. A further option would be to wrap a gift in newspaper, either sheets of newspaper or strips that have been woven together, and finish it off with a black and white or red ribbon for a dramatic effect.

You could even use wallpaper to wrap a gift, with a matching border to decorate it and make a tag. In fact, I have used lining paper as a base to the paint finishes in this book, but do bear in mind that you will only be able to use thin wallpaper or lining paper as the thicker varieties will not fold properly.

When it comes to tags and trimmings, there are many different things around you that could be used. From the garden or park you could find leaves in interesting shapes or colors to tuck under ribbon, or a fresh flower posy or single bloom to make a present even prettier. You could use cones or small bundles of twigs tied up with raffia, or even pebbles and shells if you glue them securely to the gift. In the home there is household string, wool, twine, nylon cord and braid to decorate gifts, buttons and beads to add a finishing touch, and even remnants of fabric for wrapping. However, if you are planning to use ordinary household items, take care to choose the other wrapping materials carefully to ensure you achieve a stylish and coordinated look.

Basic Wrapping Tips

When wrapping a present, there are a few useful tips which will help you achieve a perfect finish. First and foremost, always have a sharp pair of scissors and plenty of adhesive tape to hand, and work on a hard surface, not the carpet! Leave yourself plenty of time to wrap the gift, and don't attempt it just as you are leaving for the party. Try to choose a style of wrapping which is well suited to the present; for instance, you will get very disappointing and messy results if you attempt to use foil to wrap a round gift. It would be so much easier to use either tissue paper, or one of the boxes or fabric bags shown in Chapter Eight.

It is also important to ensure the wrapping is suitable for the person for whom the gift is intended. It would be inappropriate to wrap a gift for a teenage boy or elderly gentleman using pressed flowers: smart plaid paper or a burlap bag would be much better suited. The last point to consider is one of the most important if you want to achieve a good result every time. Always ensure that the gift is pre-wrapped in tissue before its final treatment. If you are wrapping in paper, this will help to smooth out sharp corners and uneven surfaces, or if you are placing the present in a giftbox or bag, you will add to the enjoyable expectation.

Household string has been used very effectively to decorate this gift. Many other unlikely materials can be used just as well.

Wrapping with Paper

There are a few special tips to consider when wrapping a gift in giftwrapping paper. First, make sure the paper is not too large for the gift or else it will create extra bulk at the corners and prevent a neat finish. Measure the gift and cut the paper down to size if necessary. Always use doublesided tape for giftwrapping. Although it is more expensive than tape which has adhesive on just one side, it allows you to stick the paper together without it showing, creating a really professional look. The last tips are to pull the paper around the gift and secure it before attempting to fold in the corners, and to tape close to the corners to prevent the paper moving while you are trying to stick it in place.

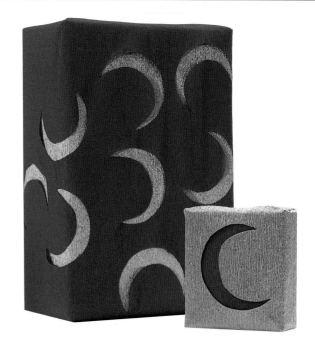

Below: Sheet music makes a simple but unusual paper to wrap a gift for a music lover. You could also try pages from comics to wrap a child's gift.

Right: Crêpe paper is now available in a huge range of colors. We have combined gold and blue here for a Christmas feel.

CHAPTER SEVEN

GIFTWRAPPING PAPERS

Papers are the obvious wrapping materials, but why not try decorating your
own, or adding finishing touches to commercial papers to make them that
little bit extra special? This section also offers alternatives to papers
that can be used in the same way for a variety of stylish effects.

Spattered Paint

1 Cut out a range of paper stars of different shapes and sizes and arrange them on the sheet of plain wrapping paper. Protect the work surface underneath with old newspaper or brown paper.

2 Using a waterbased paint, fill the brush and hold over the paper, making sure it is not too wet. Flick the bristles with your finger (which is a little messy but more effective) or the blade of a knife. Repeat with a second color on top.

3 Remove the paper stars, allow the paint to dry, wrap your present and tie it with a matching ribbon. Decorate the gift with one of the paper stars, edged with a line of paint to give it definition. Add raffia trim and glue into place.

Crêpe Crescents

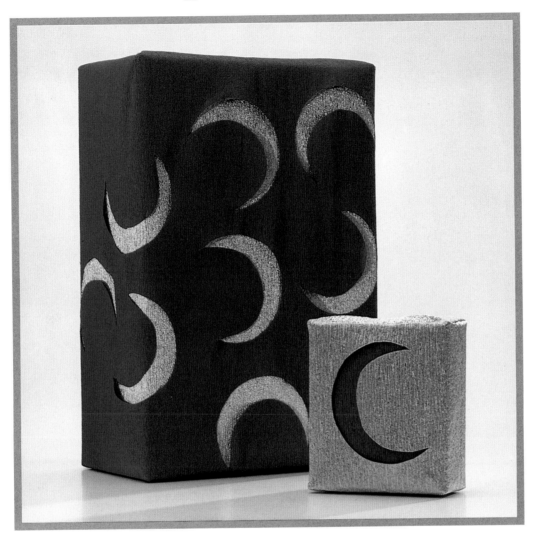

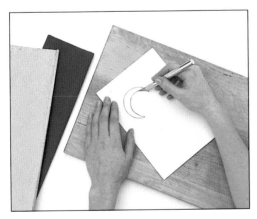

1 Choose two contrasting crêpe papers; there is now such a large variety of colors available that the combinations are endless. Draw a crescent on a piece of thin cardboard and cut it out with a craft knife to form a template.

2 Using the template, cut a series of crescent-shaped holes from the outer paper, spacing them evenly for a random effect.

3 Wrap the gift with the inner paper, then wrap again with the outer paper, taking great care not to stretch it out of shape. Use double-sided tape to secure any loose edges. Stick a strip of paper on either end to hide the cut edges.

Cellophane-wrapped Bouquet

1 You will need a round vase or jar in which to arrange the flowers. Add the flowers, one at a time, interlocking the stems in the vase as you go. Try to fan out the stems to finish with a neat spiral.

2 Tie the stems firmly together above the rim of the vase using raffia. If you are wrapping flowers with fleshy stems, like these tulips, make sure you do not cut through the stems with the raffia by tying it too tight.

3 Cut a large circle of cellophane and lay the flowers with the ends of their stems in the center. Bring the cellophane around the stems and tie with ribbon. Curl the ends of the ribbon by drawing them across the blade of the scissors.

Striped Paint Finish

1 Lay a sheet of plain paper on a protected work surface and tape it down with masking tape to prevent it from moving. Pour some emulsion paint into a bowl and water it down until it resembles thin custard.

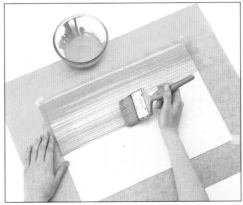

2 Dip a wide brush very lightly into the paint and wipe off the excess. Draw the brush across the paper with a steady hand, replenishing the paint as necessary. Continue until the paper is covered and leave to dry.

3 Wrap the present in the paper. To make a tag out of leftover paper, stick the paper onto thin cardboard to give it extra strength, fold in half and punch a hole in it. Attach to the gift and add a little extra decoration: we have used dried chillies.

Sheet Music

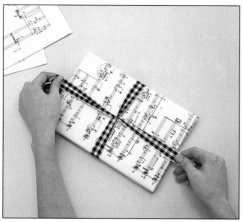

1 Wrap your gift in sheet music and tie with a contrasting ribbon.

2 Draw a musical note onto paper and use it to make a template. Cut out the note from thin black cardboard using a craft knife. Punch a hole in the top for threading the ribbon through.

3 Thread the musical note with ribbon and tie it onto the wrapped gift, finishing it with a bow.

Pressed Flower Paper

1 Choose handmade paper for this project to add to the natural appearance. Start by holding the pressed flowers carefully in one hand and removing the petals with tweezers, being very careful not to crush them.

2 Arrange the petals on the surface of the wrapped gift. Using a fine brush or toothpick, lightly dot thinned PVA glue onto the backs of the petals and stick them in place.

3 Wrap the gift in cellophane to protect the petals and tie with a raffia bow.

Ruffled Tissue

1 You will need four sheets of tissue paper. Lay the sheets of paper on top of one another, slightly off set, and gather the edges together around the gift.

2 Tie the top firmly with thin string to hold the paper in place. Then ruffle the corners to separate the layers. This will be most effective if you have used papers of different colors.

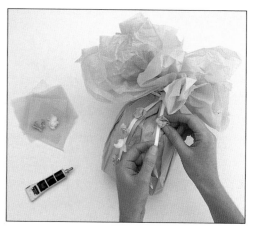

3 Take a length of braid (here we have used a shoelace) and tie it over the thin string and trim the ends. Roll small pieces of tissue into balls and glue to the braid.

Seaside Paper

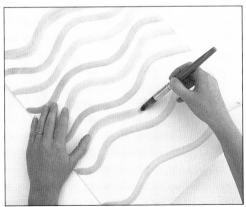

1 Lay a sheet of plain paper on the work surface and secure the corners with masking tape. Paint a series of wavy lines across the paper using blue and green poster paints. Add a few pink spots when dry.

2 Draw three fish of different sizes onto thin cardboard. Cut out and use as templates to cut six fish (two of each size) from thin cardboard, using a craft knife. Paint, allow to dry, and glue the fish onto lengths of ribbon.

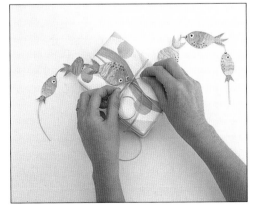

3 Wrap the gift in the painted paper and tie two lengths of plain ribbon around it. Next add the strings of fish to decorate the gift.

Corded Paper

1 Wrap the gift, using doublesided tape to secure, in a textured handmade paper. I have chosen a soft paper which resembles fabric and will combine well with the cord.

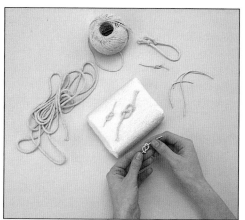

2 Take the cord or string (I have used two different thicknesses to add interest) and arrange a pattern on the gift. A series of knots or wavy lines will look effective.

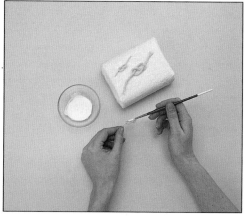

3 When the pattern is complete, paint the back of the cord with glue and press gently into place. Leave to dry. Corded paper could also be used to cover a giftbox (see page 158).

Fruit Stencils

1 Draw your design onto thin cardboard and carefully cut it out using a sharp craft knife. Remember to leave a barrier of cardboard between the cherries and the stalks so they can be painted in different colors.

2 Mask off the cherries with masking tape so you can paint the leaves. Pour the paint into a shallow dish and apply very sparingly with a stencil brush, using a circular motion. Variation in the thickness of the paint will enhance the result.

3 Remove the masking tape from the cherries and mask off the leaf and stalk areas. Carefully position the stencil over each set of leaves in turn and paint in the cherries as before, using a rich red paint.

Plaid Rosettes

1 Plaid has always been popular and there are now many plaid papers available. Wrap the gift in a plaid paper, then tie with a wide, red ribbon. Fold a length of plaid ribbon in half lengthway and tie over the top of the red ribbon.

2 To make the rosette, take a length of ribbon and sew running stitches along one edge. Pull the thread tight to gather up the ribbon.

3 Overstitch the gathered edge from the back to secure it. Then neatly sew the two ends of the ribbon together. Sew the button onto the middle of the rosette and attach to the gift.

Rococo Foil

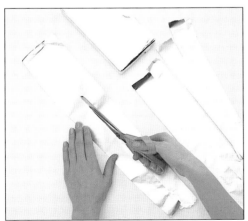

1 Wrap the gift in tin foil using double-sided tape. Cut a number of foil strips approximately 1½in (4cm) wide.

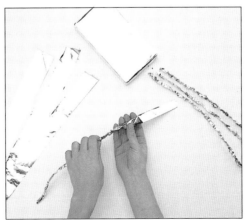

2 Lightly wrinkle the strips of foil to create textured "ribbons" and bend them into scrolls and curved shapes.

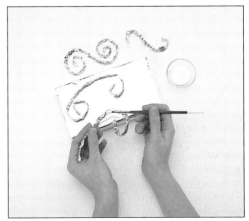

3 Carefully glue the undersides of the foil ribbons and arrange them on the gift. Push them firmly, almost flattening them, to ensure they are securely held in place.

Silver Spirals

1 Take a large sheet of plain wrapping paper and, starting from the top, fill the paper with spirals of different sizes drawn with a silver pen. Practice drawing the spirals before you begin.

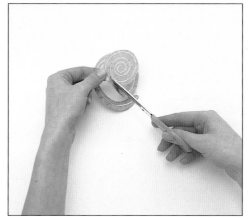

2 On a spare piece of paper, draw a large spiral and cut it out, following the line of the pen to create a paper spiral.

3 Wrap the gift in the spiral paper, tie it with silver ribbon, and slide the spiral label under the ribbon. You could create a similar effect using a gold pen and cream-colored paper.

Ragged Paper

1 You will need emulsion paint and a sheet of thick, plain paper. Bunch up a rag or cloth, dip lightly into the paint and dab over the paper, making sure you create an even coverage. Replenish the rag with paint as necessary.

2 When the blue paint is dry, repeat with the green paint and finally the light blue paint. It is a good idea to try the rag out on a spare sheet of paper before you begin. The way it has been bunched up will affect the pattern it creates.

3 Once the final coat of paint is dry, use the paper to wrap your gift. Tie the gift with cord and decorate the cord with shells glued firmly in place.

Citrus Prints

1 Cut an orange in half and dry on absorbent paper. Lightly paint the cut side with poster paint and press onto a sheet of plain paper to leave a print. Repeat to cover the paper, leave to dry, then repeat with a different color.

2 To make the decorations, cut an orange into thin slices and lay on a rack in a warm, dark place until completely dry. You can speed up the process by placing it in the bottom of a cool oven, but check it regularly to prevent burning.

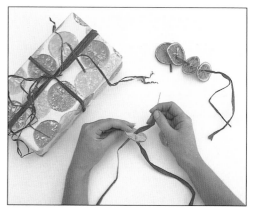

3 Wrap the gift in the paper and tie with orange raffia, leaving long ends which can be split into thinner pieces. Thread the dry orange slices onto raffia using a darning needle and knot between each slice. Tie onto the gift.

CHAPTER EIGHT

BOXES, FABRICS & BAGS

Some gifts are more difficult to wrap than others, so why not try some of the
giftboxes, fabric wrappings and giftbags in this section to make wrapping
easier? And for a special occasion, there are ideas for
using raw silk or chiffon for a luxurious effect.

Sheer Chiffon

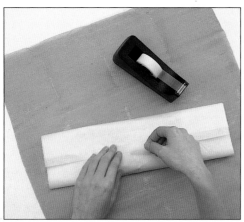

1 Wrap the gift in several layers of white tissue paper and secure with tape. Cut a piece of chiffon or organza large enough to wrap around the gift several times. Remove any selvage.

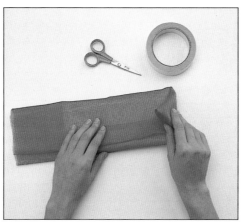

2 Wrap the fabric around the gift, fold the raw edge under itself and secure with doublesided tape. Fold the ends as you would with paper and again use doublesided tape to secure.

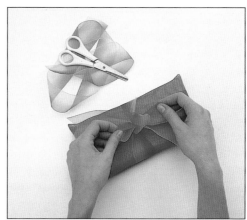

3 Finish the gift with a bow. Choose a sheer ribbon of a color which complements or contrasts with the fabric for a stunning effect.

Giftbags

1 Fold one of the long edges of a sheet of thick wrapping paper over to create a gusset and secure it with doublesided tape. Then tape along the edge to cover.

2 Place a book or small box in the center of the paper, lined up with the folded edge, and wrap the paper around it, securing the loose end as you would when wrapping a gift but leaving the folded end open. Crease along each edge.

3 Remove the book to leave an open-ended bag and press together the two creases along each side to create folds in the sides. Punch two holes in the bag along the top edge, through both thicknesses of paper, and thread with cord.

Decorated Shaker Box

1 You will need a small wooden or cardboard box; I have used a shaker-style box in a rich green. Start by trimming a piece of dry oasis foam to fit neatly into the center of the box lid, leaving a 1in (2.5cm) margin around all the sides. Glue into place and leave to dry.

2 Choose a selection of dried flowers to complement the box. We have chosen deep red strawflowers with pale green grass heads and small white flowers to set them off. Trim down the stems of the flowers to ensure they do not protrude over the rim of the box lid.

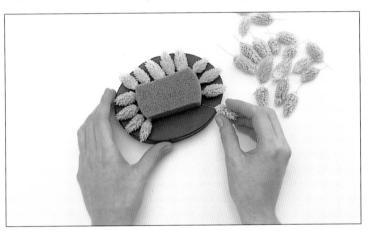

3 Start decorating the box with the grass heads, making a neat ring around the base of the foam block. Hold the heads between your thumb and forefinger and push gently into the foam with an upward movement. This will ensure the heads lie flat rather than pointing upward.

4 Add some of the small white flowers between the grass heads to ensure the foam is covered at the bottom. Push the flower stems well into the foam to cover it and to preserve the shape of the ring of grasses against the lid of the box.

5 Next add a neat row of strawflowers, selecting flower heads of a similar size and shade. Insert the flower stems close together so the foam is not visible between them.

6 Continue to add rows of flowers and grasses, leaving the grass stems progressively longer to give height further up the arrangement. Remember to fill in the gaps in the rows of grasses with the white flowers. Finish by adding one or two large strawflowers in the center.

Metallic Boxes

1 Ensure the box is clean, then apply glue around the sides to within ½in (1cm) of the box lid. Carefully stick dried split peas or lentils onto the box, flat side down, around all sides.

2 Paint glue onto the top of the box and, working from the outside edges, cover with the peas and leave to dry.

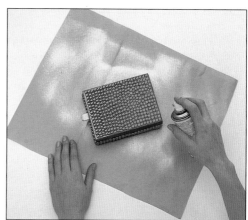

3 Protect the catch and hinges of the box with masking tape if required then spray the box with metallic paint. Apply two coats to ensure an even coverage.

Drawstring Bags

1 Cut a rectangle of fabric twice as wide as the bag you require and 2in (5cm) larger in height. Fold down a 2in (5cm) hem along the top edge, iron, and then tack in place. Cover the raw edge with binding, leaving a gap at either end and sew in place along the top and bottom edges.

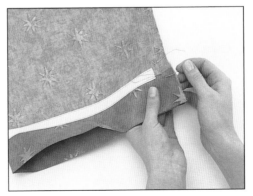

2 Make the bag shape by folding the fabric in half, right sides together, and sewing along the bottom of the bag, just in from the edge through both thicknesses of fabric. Next sew the side seam, right up to the top, but leaving a gap in the seam where the binding comes.

3 Turn the bag out and press the side seam. Fold under the raw edges of the seam and slipstitch in place, making sure the opening near the binding is still clear. Thread the cord or ribbon through the binding using a large needle. Bring the ends through the seam opening and tie.

Christmas Box

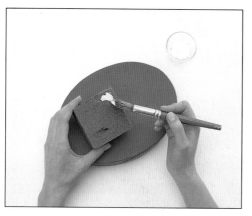

1 Cut a piece of dry oasis foam to fit the lid of the box, leaving a 2in (5cm) margin around the sides. Glue into place and leave to dry.

2 Cut a number of florist's wires in half to leave them about 4in (10cm) long and bend in half to create large staples. Use these to pin a length of green tinsel to the oasis foam in a spiral. Make sure the foam is not visible through the tinsel.

3 Twist a wire around the base of each Christmas tree decoration, and insert the free end into the foam through the tinsel, ensuring that there are no sharp ends protruding out. Add decorations until the lid is complete.

Raw Silk Bow

1 Wrap the gift in raw silk, sewing it into place. Cut two pieces of silk 30x4in (75x10cm) and one piece 13x2½in (33x6cm). Fold the small piece in half, right sides together. Sew along both long sides, turn through and slipstitch the raw end.

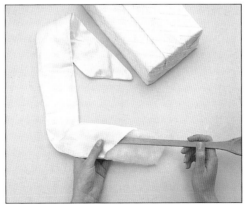

2 Arrange the other pieces together, right sides facing, and stitch both long sides. Stitch a diagonal seam at the end to create the points of the bow. Turn through and press. Lightly stuff the bow with interlining and slipstitch the open end.

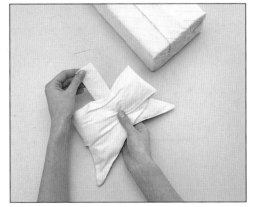

3 Fold the padded silk to create the bow as shown. Wrap the small piece around the center to create the knot and slipstitch the ends together at the back. Sew some artificial flowers onto the gift and sew the bow on top.

Paper-covered Boxes

1 Cut the paper so it covers the base and sides of the box and protrudes into the inside by 1½in (4cm) all round. Fix a strip of doublesided tape to the top and bottom edges of each long side. Place the box in the center of the paper and mark, then crease, along one of the long edges.

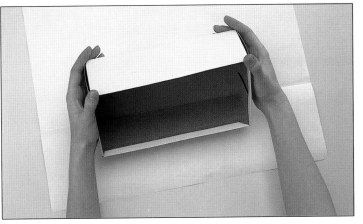

2 Peel the backing off the doublesided tape. Keeping the bottom edge of the box on the crease line on the paper, carefully bring the box down on its side and press to ensure the paper has stuck. Turn the box over, pulling the paper tightly across the base, and repeat with the other side.

3 Make cuts from the long edges of the paper to each of the box corners. Stick a piece of doublesided tape along one side of the box inside and fold the paper over into the box and stick it in place. Repeat with the other side.

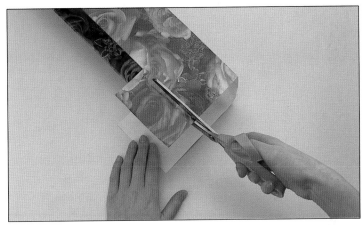

4 To cover the ends of the box, first cut the excess paper away from each box corner to the edge of the sheet. It is easier to lay the box on its side to do this.

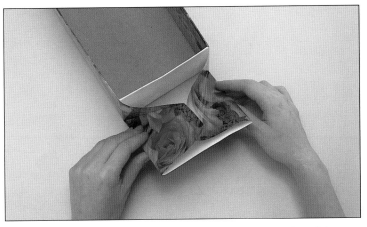

5 Make a light crease from the bottom corner to the top edge of the paper on either side. Fold the extra paper into the middle as shown in the picture and bring the flap up the side of the box, firming the creases as you go. The top of the flap should fold over into the box.

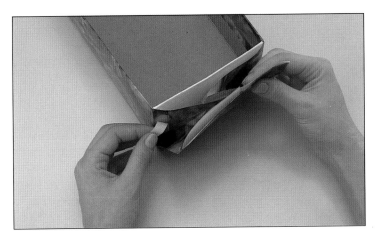

6 Stick a strip of doublesided tape on the outer rim of the box and stick the paper to it, then stick another piece between the two layers of paper on either side, as shown. Press the paper into place. Then stick the end of the flap inside the box with more tape. Repeat to cover the lid of the box.

Puffy Paint Parcels

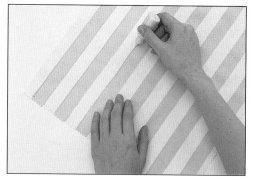

1 To achieve this particular effect, you will need a striped fabric but you can of course use puffy paint on any fabric, highlighting the patterns in different ways. Cut out a rectangle of fabric using pinking shears, then paint a line of puffy paint along the edge of each stripe.

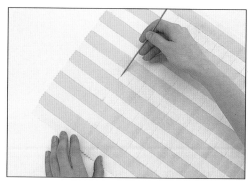

2 Before the paint dries, take a wooden skewer or cocktail stick and score across the lines of paint at right angles to create a feathered effect. Leave the paint to dry, then follow the manufacturer's instructions to puff the paint; it will usually require some form of heat.

3 Wrap the gift in the usual way using tape. If you are wrapping a cylinder-shaped gift, gather the ends evenly at the top and tie with ribbon to complement or contrast with the fabric. Because the fabric was cut with pinking shears, you will not need to hem the edges.

Pyramids

1 Wrap the gift loosely in colored tissue paper. Draw an equilateral triangle onto a sheet of thin colored cardboard and cut it out. The length of each side should be twice the height you need the box to be. Punch a hole in each point.

2 Make a mark halfway along each side of the triangle. Take each point in turn, and fold it across to the opposite side of the triangle to line up with the mark; make a sharp crease. Fold the points up to make a three-dimensional triangle.

3 Thread ribbon through the holes in the points, put the gift inside and tighten the ribbon to close the parcel. Finish with a bow.

Pretty Fabric Cases

1 Cut out a piece of fabric the same length but twice the width you want the case to be, remembering to add a little all around as a seam allowance. Cut out another two strips of fabric twice the width you want the finished case to be and about 3in (8cm) wide.

2 Cut eight pieces of fabric tape or ribbon and pin, then tack, along the long edges of the fabric, which will be the ends of the case when the fabric is folded. Arrange four on each side so they will match up and form the ties when the case is complete.

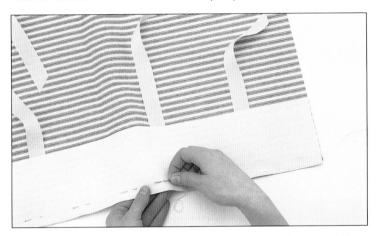

3 Lay the two strips of fabric on top of the main rectangle, one on either side with right sides facing. Pin, tack, and stitch along the outside edges, enclosing the ties between them as you go. Press the seams open with an iron.

4 Next, fold the fabric in half, right sides facing, to form the shape of the case, matching the ties down either side. Sew along the open edge and press the seam open.

5 Turn the case through with the main seam down one edge and press. Tuck the ends of the fabric inside so that the seams holding the extra strips of fabric in place are approximately 1in (2.5cm) from the ends inside the case. The ties should protrude from the ends of the case.

6 Slipstitch along the seam inside to keep the casing in place. Slip the gift in the case and fasten the ties. This is a lovely way to wrap a special gift. The case could be used afterward by the recipient as a nightdress case or as a drawer freshener filled with potpourri.

Scented Basket

1 This is a pretty way of giving a basket of toiletries, making each item look special. Wrap the soap in a square of muslin and tie with a piece of natural cord. Wrap some bath foam balls in a colored net parcel, and fold a face cloth into quarters, tie with ribbon, and finish with a flower.

2 Fill the basket with tissue paper, chosen to complement the color scheme, and arrange the toiletries on top. You could also include a natural sponge, a wooden-handled hairbrush or nailbrush and a selection of shells in the basket for added interest.

3 Once you are happy with the arrangement of the items inside the basket, take a large square of clear cellophane. Stand the basket in the center of the cellophane, and bring the corners up over the handle of the basket. Secure with an elastic band, then finish with a ribbon.

Glitter Glue Boxes

1 Tear out two squares of handmade paper in different colors to fit on the lid of the box, one on top of the other to create a staggered effect. See page 180 for instructions on how to tear handmade paper. Glue the larger square on the lid.

2 Draw a wavy sun design on a piece of tracing paper, then when you are happy with the shape, transfer it onto the smaller square of handmade paper.

3 Using a gold glitter glue pen, draw over the top of the pencil lines to leave a glittery gold star on the paper. Leave to dry, then stick the paper to the lid of the box, on top of the other square.

Card Photograph Wallet

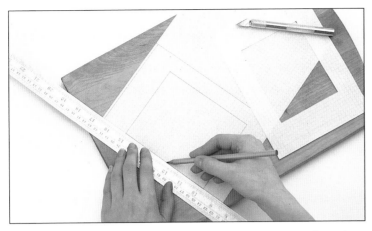

1 Cut out two pieces of paper 8x6in (20x15cm), then cut out the centers to make templates for the two frames. The first frame should be 1¼in (3cm) wide at the sides and 1¾in (4cm) at top and bottom; the second frame should be 1in (2.5cm) each side and 1½in (3.5cm) top and bottom.

2 Using the second template, cut out a frame from cream corrugated paper, making sure the corrugations run vertically. Cut out a rectangle from the same paper 12¼x8in (30.5x20cm). This will form the wallet itself and will be folded in half to make the finished item 8x6in (20x15cm).

3 Using the first template, cut out a frame from a paper of a contrasting color, with the corrugations running horizontally. We have used a terracotta shade. This frame will be positioned behind the pale one to make a contrasting-colored margin in the center around the photograph.

4 Cut two pieces of fabric tape or ribbon and glue one to each side of the wallet, at the center of each inside edge. These will be the ties to hold the wallet closed so they must line up when the wallet is folded.

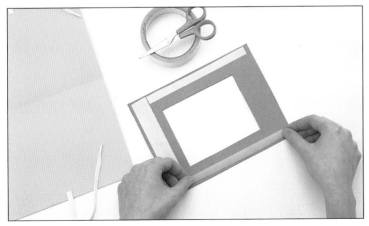

5 Stick strips of doublesided tape down both sides and along the bottom of the terracotta frame. Position this frame inside the wallet on the right-hand side. Make sure the tape is not too close to the inside edges of the frame as it may stop the photograph from sliding into place.

6 Using doublesided tape on all sides, stick the pale frame on top of the darker one. Cut a thin strip of cream paper and stick on the inside left-hand edge of the wallet to hide the end of the tie. This wallet will fit a photograph 5x4in (12.5x10cm); adjust the measurements if necessary.

Gift Sacks

1 Cut a rectangle of burlap, fold in half and sew along the bottom and up the side to create a bag. Turn through and press. Leave the top edge unfinished so you can fray the edges by pulling out the burlap threads one by one.

2 Cut the letters of the recipient's name out of fabric and glue onto a piece of leather or other fabric cut with a decorative edge. Once dry, glue the leather onto the burlap bag.

3 Braid three long pieces of natural twine and finish in a large knot at either end. Fray out the ends of the string, place the gift in the bag and tie the top with the twine braid.

Cord-covered Jars

1 Spread glue around the bottom of the jar and stick the end of the cord in place. Wrap the cord firmly around the jar, adding more glue as necessary and leaving no space between rows.

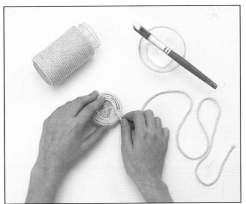

2 When the jar is complete, use the same method to cover the lid starting at the rim and working up the sides and toward the center. Run two extra rows around the rim to define the lid.

3 Add contrasting cord or a few shells as a final decoration, fixing them with strong glue. This method is suitable for covering jars and cans, or could even be used on conventional giftboxes.

Calico Hearts

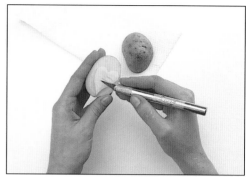

1 Etch a heart shape onto the cut face of half a potato and cut away the surrounding potato. Using a sharp knife, score a few wavy broken lines through the heart, making sure some of them start at the edges. This will give a textured appearance when printed.

2 Dab the potato with absorbant paper to dry. Apply the paint of your choice sparingly onto the potato using a brush. Print hearts onto the fabric, replenishing the paint as necessary. Always practice first to find the amount of paint required to give the effect you want. Allow to dry.

3 Cut the calico to the size required and wrap the gift using doublesided tape to secure. An easy and effective way to make a tag is to cut out a small scrap of calico and glue onto thin card. Trim to size when dry, punch a hole in one corner, and attach onto the gift with ribbon.

CHAPTER NINE

FINISHING TOUCHES

Gift tags and trimmings can enhance any gift, giving it a personal touch and
making it a little more special without taking too much time and effort.
These finishing touches will brighten up many different gifts and can be adapted
to suit the style and color of the giftwrapping paper or fabric used.

Wax Seal

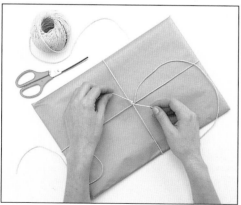

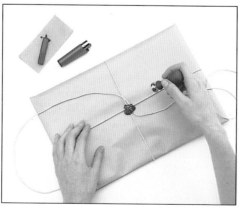

1 In earlier days, a wax seal was the only way of sealing a parcel for security and although a little tricky, it does finish off the parcel in a very stylish way. Wrap the gift and tie with string, finishing with a knot at the front of the parcel.

2 Melt a stick of sealing wax over a naked flame and drip wax over and around the knot on the gift. Before the wax hardens, press your stamp down firmly into it. It may be advisable to practice elsewhere before you try it on your gift.

3 Make a label from a piece of leftover paper and decorate it with another seal. Punch a hole in the corner, write your message inside, and attach to one of the loose ends of string on the gift.

Salt Dough Tags

1 Mix 4 tablespoons of plain white flour, 2 tablespoons of salt, $\frac{1}{2}$ tablespoon of vegetable oil, and 4 tablespoons of water in a bowl. Knead until you have a smooth, firm dough. Remove from the bowl and knead for a further five minutes.

2 Roll the dough out onto a floured board to about $\frac{1}{4}$in ($\frac{1}{2}$cm) thick. Cut out shapes with a cookie cutter or knife, make a hole in the top of each with the end of a drinking straw and transfer to a lined cookie sheet.

3 Bake the labels in a cool oven for about two hours and leave until completely cold. Paint them with acrylic paint and when dry, varnish on both sides. Thread ribbon through the hole in the top and tie to the gift.

Tissue Paper Flowers

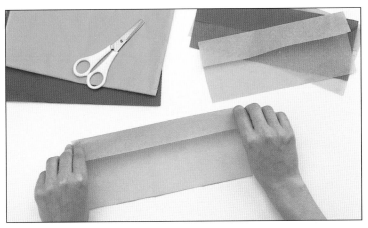

1 These simple, inexpensive flowers can be used to enhance any parcel. Cut some strips of tissue paper about 10x6in (25x15cm), depending on how large you wish the flowers to be. Fold about one third of the paper over lengthway to prevent the flower stalk from becoming too bulky.

2 Tuck one corner of the folded edge in and gather and roll up the tissue paper strip, turning the flower in your hand as you progress. When you have finished, tuck the loose corner in as before.

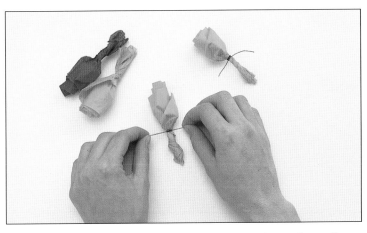

3 Twist the base of the flower two or three times to form a firm stalk. Bind the stalk tightly with thread and tie securely. Repeat with as many flowers as you need.

4 A number of green tissue paper leaves can be made to complement and set off the flowers. Cut out squares of green tissue approximately 4in (10cm) across and fold down both corners along the top edge to make a point. Leave the bottom corners as they are.

5 Bring the two sides of the leaf together, with the point in the center, holding the edges as shown. Gather the tissue paper tightly with the thumb and finger of one hand and open up the leaf with the other, straightening out the edges. Secure the stalk with thread as before.

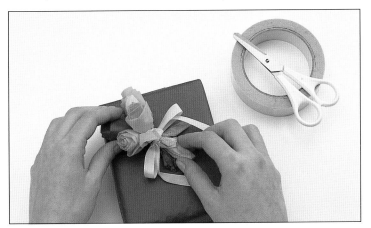

6 Arrange the flowers and leaves into a neat posy and tie them together with thread. Hide the thread with a neat bow of ribbon and stick the posy to the gift with doublesided tape.

Curled Pipe Cleaners

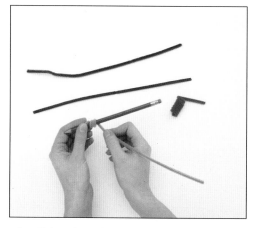

1 Select about eight pipe cleaners (also called chenille stems) for each gift. To curl them, hold the end of one against a pencil and wrap it tightly around the pencil in a neat spiral.

2 Slip the pencil out of the pipe cleaner and adjust the length of the pipe cleaner by pulling firmly on the ends.

3 Attach the pipe cleaners to the gift by wrapping the straight ends around the ribbon or rickrack in the center of the gift. Add small balloons, if required, to add to the fun.

Pressed Flower Tag

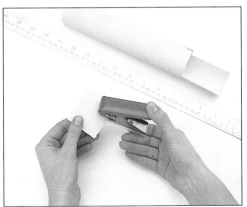

1 You can press flowers at home in a heavy book; they will take two to four weeks to dry. I have used a heavy-duty lining paper to make this tag. Tear (rather than cut) a rectangle from the paper and fold in half. Punch a hole in the corner.

2 Gently lift the pressed flowers onto the label. Once you have arranged them, stick in place by dotting glue onto the back of the flowers with a fine brush or toothpick. Once dry, protect the flowers with a coat of aerosol varnish.

3 Finish the tag by painting a fine line around the edge in a complementary color. Thread ribbon through the hole and attach to the gift.

Feathers & Braids

1 Take six pieces of wool, two each of three different colors, and wrap around the parcel leaving the ends long for braiding. I have used green felt to wrap the gift, making an interesting alternative to paper.

2 Braid the loose ends, using both strands of the same color together to make a thicker braid. Secure the braids with a knot and unravel the ends to make a tassel. Slip feathers into the braids and hold in place with a little glue.

3 To make a label, cut three identical triangles from colored card. Glue on top of each other, offset to give a staggered effect. Trim along the bottom edge of the highest triangle to leave three triangles of different sizes. Punch a hole.

Beaded Boxes

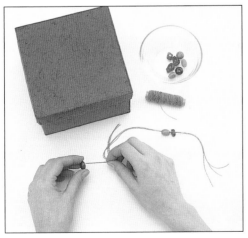

1 Cut six pieces of green elastic to fit around the box. Thread three pieces onto a needle and thread on the beads.

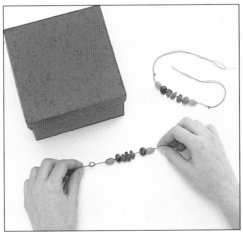

2 Repeat with the other pieces. Make a large knot on either side of the beads on both pieces to stop them from moving along the elastic.

3 Tie the elastic around the giftbox, pulling it tight and knotting underneath. Trim the ends of the elastic.

Botanical Tag

1 Handmade paper looks much better if it has been torn rather than cut. Mark out the tag on the paper in pencil and wet along the line using a ruler and wet paintbrush. Leave it to soak for a minute, then carefully tear along the wet line, holding the ruler down on one side as you go.

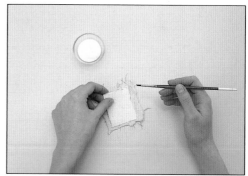

2 Tear out two squares of paper for the tag, one a little smaller than the other. Choose a relatively pale color, such as cream or white, for the smaller square so your painting will show up clearly. Glue the small square of paper on top of the larger one.

3 Using watercolors and a fine brush, paint a simple botanical subject on the front. If you are not an experienced painter, just paint a single flower; it can be as simple as you like. Punch a hole in the corner of the tag and thread with raffia. Attach to the gift.

Fan Decorations

1 Choose a paper to either match or contrast with the paper in which you have wrapped the gift. Cut a strip of paper the width of your gift and about three times the width long. Fold it in half widthway, then fold into small, neat pleats starting at the folded end.

2 When you have pleated the whole length, fold the closed fan in half. Stick the two loose edges in the center together to create a solid fan with a flat base. Make sure you stick the edges tightly together down their entire length so the join cannot be seen when the fan is open.

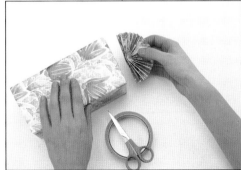

3 Open the fan out, pulling the sides down until the base is flat. Apply doublesided tape to the base of the fan and stick it to the top of the gift so it stands up straight. You could also add a second, smaller fan in a different color for a very professional effect.

Natural Choice

1 Wrap your gift in a natural, hand-made paper which will complement the trimmings, using doublesided tape to secure it. Cut a strip of corrugated paper about one quarter the width of the gift and long enough to go right around it.

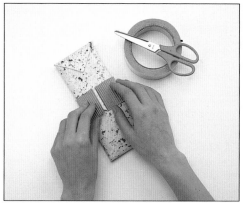

2 Wrap the corrugated paper around the middle of the gift and secure it neatly at the back using doublesided tape.

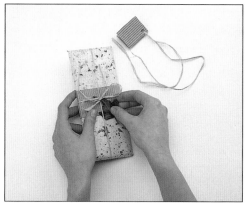

3 Finish by tying with raffia; secure it with a neat bow, and slip a leaf under it. You could also add a simple tag. Cut a rectangle from corrugated paper, fold in half to make a small card, punch a hole in one corner and attach to the gift.

Bright Buttons

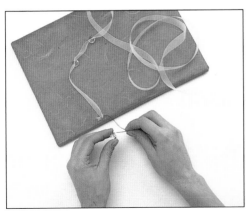

1 Select buttons with either a single hole or large holes; they are easier to position once threaded. Attach a needle and thread to the end of a piece of ribbon and thread the buttons on, choosing the number and style to suit the gift.

2 An additional sleeve of giftwrapping paper has been wrapped around the gift to add interest. Simply cut a rectangle, slightly narrower than the gift, wrap around the gift, fold the edge back on itself and secure with doublesided tape.

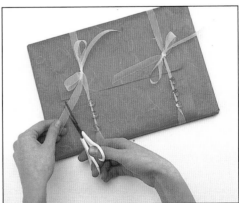

3 Tie the ribbon around the gift and position the buttons by sliding them up and down the ribbon as necessary. The green gift has the addition of two paper leaves. Cut the shapes from paper and secure with doublesided tape.

Raffia Trimmings

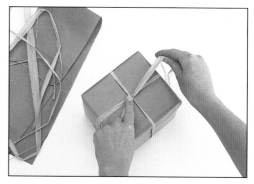

1 Plain brown paper complements the natural look of these decorations. Wrap the gift in a double layer of brown paper and secure with doublesided tape. Take two pieces of raffia and tie around the gift, leaving the loose ends long on top of the parcel.

2 Take three ears of dried wheat and a long piece of curly willow and arrange them together in a little posy. Secure the stems together with florist's wire. Tie a short piece of raffia around the stems a number of times to hide the wire.

3 Place the posy on top of the gift and tie it in place with the long raffia ends. Finish with a neat bow. You could vary this idea in any number of ways by using colored raffia, for example, and adding a few colorful dried flowers or other grasses to the posy.

Fresh Flower Posy

1 Choose a few fresh flowers to make the posy, selecting only perfect blooms. The flowers you choose will greatly affect the look of the gift so select carefully. Arrange them into a neat posy and fix with an elastic band. Trim the stems.

2 Wind a piece of florist's tape around the stems over the elastic band to hold them together more securely.

3 Attach the flowers to the wrapped gift by winding ribbon around the stems and then around the gift. Finish with a bow. Trim the ends of the ribbon to length.

Découpage Tags

1 Cut out motifs from old greeting cards or sheets of giftwrapping paper. We have chosen a flower theme. Cut around the edges very carefully, varying the sizes and colors you choose.

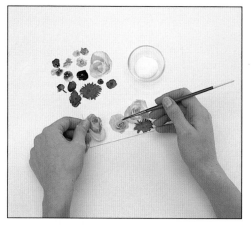

2 Cut out a rectangle of paper or thin cardboard to make the label. Position the flowers onto it and glue into place.

3 Attach the label to your gift with glue. We have used thin paper ribbon to edge the label and give it a more finished appearance.

Tassels

1 Tassels can be made from wool, thread, string, or raffia. Cut a piece of thin cardboard to the size you would like the tassel to be. Wind a length of raffia around and around the card until you have achieved the required thickness.

2 Tie the loops of raffia tightly together at the top of the card using another piece of raffia. Cut through the loops at the bottom of the card to leave a tuft of loose ends.

3 Wrap a short length of raffia around the middle of the tassel about ¾in (2cm) from the top and tie tightly. Trim the ends to form a neat bunch and tie the tassel to the gift.

Index